PERSUASIVE
FICTIONS

PERSUASIVE FICTIONS

Feminist Narrative and Critical Myth

Anna Wilson

Lewisburg
Bucknell University Press
London: Associated University Presses

Associated University Presses
440 Forsgate Drive
Cranbury, NJ 08512

Associated University Presses
16 Barter Street
London WC1A 2AH, England

Associated University Presses
P.O. Box 338, Port Credit
Mississauga, Ontario
Canada L5G 4L8

The paper used in this publication meets the requirements of the American National Standard for Permanence of Paper for Printed Library Materials Z39.48-1984.

Library of Congress Cataloging-in-Publication Data

Wilson, Anna, 1954–
    Persuasive fictions : feminist narrative and critical myth / Anna Wilson.
        p.   cm.
    Includes bibliographical references and index.
    ISBN 0-8387-5482-1 (alk. paper)
    1. American literature—Women authors—History and criticism.
    2. Feminism and literature—United States—History—20th century.
    3. Feminism and literature—England—History—18th century.   4. American literature—20th century—History and criticism.   5. Wollstonecraft, Mary, 1759–1797—Criticism and interpretation.   6. Lorde, Audre—Criticism and interpretation.   7. French, Marilyn, 1929– Women's room.   8. Feminism and motion pictures.   9. Rape in motion pictures.   10. Women and literature.   11. Women in literature.   12. Narration (Rhetoric) I. Title.
    PS228.F45   W55   2001
    813'.5099287—dc21

                                                                00-065129

Contents

Prologue: The Origin Story

It's a big party, everyone's there. As the guests come in they are greeted by those who arrived earlier, they haven't seen each other since the last conference, there's years of gossip to squeeze into a moment. The group around the crib is especially loud, these witches always are. They barely remember not to spill their drinks on the blanket. The ceremony is about to begin: the baby's Spirit of Creativity raps her wand on the changing table and points at the witch to her right.

The first witch's teeth sparkle in the lamplight like diamonds: "I give you, O Feminist Writer of the Future, a Bestseller so that you may live in comfort and send your children to private schools."

The second witch doesn't waste a moment; she must have been expecting something of the sort: "And I, little one, give you an Early Experimental Text which will eventually be canonized!" She smiles in triumph. A murmur of appreciation ripples through the audience.

The third witch is leaning heavily on her cane; her smile is twisted and her voice is the rasping of a saw. "I bequeath you a rich legacy, one that many before you have enjoyed and profited from"—in the silence, the baby can be heard gurgling trustfully. "I give you the hatred and opprobrium of male critics!"

This causes quite a stir. The Spirit of Creativity is heard to mutter, "Oh really, Mary, why did you have to pass *that* on? *So* second-wave separatist," in tones of exasperation. A hundred conversations break out at once as to the psychic consequences to the poor baby of all those attacks on her self-esteem.

Old witch three draws herself up: "Give her something to fight against," she intones, and turns back into the crowd to get herself another martini. It's a cash bar, but the witches are on expenses.

The fourth witch is flicking anxiously through her index cards; does she have anything remedial? It's annoying, having to rescue things when she had wanted to add a challenging, experimental touch. The Spirit is swishing her wand backwards and forwards impatiently. "Oh, all right," the witch says, "you had better have the whole-hearted attention, respect, and appreciation of feminist critics." The Spirit lifts an eyebrow. "And feminist readers," the witch adds, blushing.

Things deteriorate a little after that. Various other, less powerful, witches come up and offer the baby useful qualities: long life, painful love affairs, stays at writers' colonies. The Spirit and the main witches retreat to the bar to argue about who gets to go first, and whether the order of gifts makes any difference to the future outcome anyway. Gradually the party drifts into other parts of the room. The crib is left unattended. No one is looking when a guest detaches herself from a knot of people and wanders over to the baby. She leans over and whispers in the baby's ear: "I've got something else for you. Here it is: the Inevitable Failure of Your Work to Change the World." A faint crease forms on the baby's brow; perhaps she emits a quiet whimper. The last witch straightens. She pats the baby's stomach comfortingly. "But don't worry," she says, "no one will ever notice that you have this gift. It's our secret."

PERSUASIVE
FICTIONS

Introduction: The Use of Blunt Instruments

The Problem of Belief

Feminist criticism is a suspicious activity. From its earliest manifestations, typified by Judith Fetterley's resisting reader, skepticism and a disinclination to believe what one's told have been enabling qualities for the feminist critic.[1] She is trained, whatever her other theoretical tendencies, in a hermeneutics of suspicion. Nonetheless—and perhaps partly in reaction to the habit of doubt, but more particularly because feminist criticism even now acknowledges a contested linkage to an activist past—there are some articles of feminist faith.[2] The one that concerns me here is our belief in the power of the text.

Of course, all readers ascribe to various versions of this received notion, that texts somehow have the power not merely to reflect but also to shape the world or at least the individual's sense of her place in it. There are important differences in the ways this idea is both theorized and acted upon; while a conspicuous and sometimes influential segment of American readers believes that people become what they read, the process of causal mimesis which turns readers of *The Adventures of Huckleberry Finn* or viewers of *Natural Born Killers* into amoral deviants, others grant less direct power to texts but still assume that the encounter between reader and word and image is a potentially interactive one.[3] Were this not the case, the early 1970s' "images of women" criticism, based on the identification of stereotypes and positive and negative portrayals of women in literature, would have made no sense—but neither would more current critical activities focused on textual performativity of gender or subject position.

But in addition to the general agreement that texts matter, and matter in material ways, we can identify, and probably acquiesce fairly comfortably in, another proposition: that some texts matter more than others. One can imagine various criteria, depending on one's current purpose, for selection and taxonomy here: canonical position, representative merit (conveying something about the experience of being an Italian-American immigrant in nineteenth-century New York, for example), power to enlighten (or perhaps blight), and so on. My focus, one that seems to me an important area for further consideration for feminist criticism, is texts that matter because they have instrumental power: paradigmatically, books that change lives. While, again, the idea of a particular work as profoundly influential on the individual, for good or ill, is culturally normative, there is a specific valence to the feminist belief in textual power, that of the capacity of some texts to be not only individually but *politically* transformative. Not only, that is, can books change an individual life, they can act on social systems.[4]

Given the existence of the instrumental text, an important critical task becomes to find and define it, asking whatever formally directed questions supply clues as to its type. From the question of Which text? one might then go on to address supplementary ones such as How does it work? and Whom does it work upon? All these, in various degrees, have been the object of feminist study, as I discuss below.

But I want to ask a different question and open up a different series of inquiries. This question, one that, for all the historicizing and self-reflexive work now happening in feminist criticism, does not seem to get asked, is *Is* there an effective instrumental text? (And if so, what are the material conditions necessary for its operation?) The works of fiction and film that I will discuss in depth in the chapters that follow are, or try to be, instrumental in the sense that they are overtly politically engaged, seeking to change the reading and viewing audience on a more than personally transformative level. By examining how a series of texts has sought instrumentality, looking in detail at the reception of these texts as well as at how the works present themselves as legible or available to be read, I hope to show that texts have a lot less power in the world than one might suppose, and that such instrumentality as they do possess, rather than being embedded within the text itself, is a condition of the particular historical location within which reading happens. I will argue that "resistance" is fragile, local, and fluid, existing in a necessarily impermanent confluence of text, reader, and social context, and that its power to move beyond the individual into the social is still more a question of contingent conditions, if possible at all. This suggestion raises, in its turn, another question: If the instrumental text is not so effective after all, how to account for the critical investment in the notion that (feminist) books change (women's) lives? When individual texts are studied in the context of their original reception, it becomes apparent that oppositional power is often a reading effect produced by critical hindsight. Who benefits, then, from the belief in the feminist instrumental text as it is wielded critically or institutionally? Would destabilizing this belief have important theoretical or pedagogical consequences for feminism?

Many critical works have recently been written on contemporary women's fiction, and of these several of the most persuasive pay particular attention to the consciousness-raising texts of the 1970s, both in literary terms and as agent of social change. The overarching focus of these studies is the formal properties of texts; and accordingly the conversations between one critic and another that such studies enact, directly or indirectly, are conversations, for example, about the subversive capacities of postmodernism versus the metafictional elements of realism, or the relative merits of rival chronologies of rise and decline.[5] These are important and interesting conversations, and these various works make significant interventions that both influence and comment upon the continuing process of feminist canon formation. But because the terms of the argument essentially revolve around the problem of which texts, and which forms of text, to valorize as feminist fiction, interrogation of the social activity of text in and upon the world tends to get sidelined. Thus for many critics the transformative properties of the feminist text are simply taken for granted, the ground from which they begin their project. So Marie Lauret opens her *Liberating Literature* (1994) with a typical assertion:

> Books do change lives. This book is about the role of literature in social movements, about fiction that has designs upon its readers, about writing that changed the lives of individual women by giving them a sense of collectivity, of movement, and a vision of social change. Books . . . helped to bring about the profound social changes effected by the Women's Movement.[6]

Gayle Greene makes a similar authorizing claim in *Changing the Story* (1991), based on her own experience of coming to feminist consciousness through a reading of *The Golden Notebook*.[7] Rita Felski's nuanced and subtle account of the "feminist public sphere" in *Beyond Feminist Aesthetics* (1989), a work in which she is explicitly concerned to render visible the institutions that enable and control literary production, assumes without analysis the instrumental power of mimesis. Felski's project is to revalidate realist fiction as the site of effective political engagement, displacing the avant-garde forms that others have privileged. So although she puts production and reception back into the foreground of the critical picture, her argument is still finally a textual one, replacing one form with another.

Ellen Cronan Rose raises several pertinent questions in her 1993 *Signs* review essay on works in the field, including whether changes in form alone are sufficient to promote changes in the reader.[8] She points out that the universalized "woman reader" who tends to feature as a transcultural ideal in these works is in fact based on a particular generationally specific experience and type—that of the critic's own.[9] Cora Kaplan and Lisa Hogeland have also historicized the reader who is transformed by the feminist text. Kaplan locates the capacity to change in an activist past, before the creation of a feminist literary critical institution. In "Feminist Criticism Twenty Years On," she contrasts the current reading of feminist texts with their use in the 1970s; whereas contemporary critics are "cut off" from cultural and imaginative practice, novels were then read as "part of the ongoing debate of the social movement of which we were part."[10]

In her recent study *Feminism and Its Fictions* (1998), Hogeland argues that not only was the reading scene of the '70s a specific and unrecoverable location, the consciousness-raising text was itself an historically specific form. Hogeland's perception that "feminist reading" (the kind that causes one to see the world, and oneself in it, differently) is not universal and timeless but a specific effect produced by consciousness-raising novels in the '70s is an important contribution to focusing attention on reception as a founding condition of whether, and how, change happens. But her account elides the difference and the difficulty of establishing a connection between individual and social transformation.[11] Thus these novels can become the "high renaissance" of feminist activism in her account, despite Hogeland's own incisive critique of such texts as increasingly focused on promotion of individual self-worth rather than on changing the world outside the reader.[12]

Rose's essay, with its marked skepticism about the transformative properties of the texts privileged by feminist critics and now becoming part of an established canon, is one indication of the beginnings of apostasy from feminist faith. Hogeland's work seems to auger a further shift, for while Rose limits herself to suggesting that different texts and canons may be needed for the transformation of different readers, *Feminism and Its Fictions* challenges the supreme power of the feminist word:

> Feminist criticism's utopian project of total social transformation rested on an enormous faith in the power of texts to make change. That faith in turn rested on a belief in feminist literacy *as* social change: providing new ways of mirroring and creating women's identity could transform culture only insofar as "your mind" was the real battleground of feminism.[13]

My own project of inquiry into the status of the instrumental text pushes this tendency further, taking up what seem to me its implications. I seek to move away from the search for an oppositional form, from the idea that resistance can be located in the formal properties of a text, which turns that text into a kind of feminist Certs, a pill the reader in search of radicalization can slip under her tongue any time and in any place. And rather than search for that ideal historical moment when individual and social transformation happened simultaneously—the instrumental text's dream of perfect harmony—I propose instead to inquire into specific, local, encounters between texts and audiences. My study focuses on works that both present themselves and have been received as politically effective. While I include in this project a novel from the 1970s, the currently privileged location of feminist instrumental texts, I begin with an analysis of Mary Wollstonecraft, who functions as a monument of feminist opposition in contemporary criticism: in this iconic role, she is exemplary of a signifier of resistance that has become detached from its history, and from the history of her texts and their historical reception.

I also move away from an exclusive focus on fiction as the genre of oppositional production, a move motivated in part by the shift of focus from form to effect—where the latter is the starting point, it is obvious that film is potentially an important twentieth-century medium of influence that needs to be considered. In addition, the traditional concentration on novels and autobiography in the literature on feminist interventions is to some degree a consequence of the absence of a significant body of women film directors, given that a female authorial signature has been a necessary precondition for comfortable insertion under the rubric "feminist."[14] Again, if change is to be foregrounded as that which is to be searched for, the gender of the director is less than central as a defining factor.[15] While feminist films directed by women may well be qualitatively different in cinematic technique or effect on an audience (and will almost certainly be differently funded and distributed), Jonathan Kaplan's *The Accused* (1988) qualifies for my purposes as a feminist text by virtue of its announced intention to address feminist issues, and its reception history.

The skepticism that I began by claiming as fundamental to feminist critical activity, and by reclaiming as the guiding force behind my own intervention, is easier to inhabit in a supposedly "postfeminist" historical moment. The current debate in feminist criticism about the value of privileging gender as an organizing device (whether of oppression or resistance, of authors, or readers) suggests the degree to which at least some practitioners are moving away from the old certainties and beliefs.[16] That the debate continues heatedly also evidences the continued power and force of gender as means to identity, theory, and action. By including Kaplan's film within the definition of a feminist instrumental text, I am privileging feminist engagement (successful or otherwise) over either gender essence or identity. This is still, of course, to some extent a de facto privileging of gender, since "feminist" clearly has a gender-specific historical resonance. For my purposes, however, feminist criticism remains an historical (and actual) phenomenon worth studying, both for what such study can suggest about what feminist critics might best be doing now, and because a theory of the instrumental text's operations in culture is relevant to any politically engaged critical position. This study's focus on (mostly) female-authored texts and (mostly) white-authored texts arises then from its subject, not from my personal or political commitment to gender or whiteness over other defining rubrics. I am making an argument about a particular kind of historically inflected feminist process: the creation of the idea of the feminist instrumental text and its operations within feminist criticism.[17]

The answer to the question, Who benefits from the idea of successful instrumental text? is on one level simple: we feminist critics do. It justifies our existence. But I am not suggesting that I drag myself out of bed and into the classroom, rather than down to the barricades, because I believe that *The Women's Room* will infect my students with revolutionary fervor. Nor do I believe that other feminist critics are prey to such self-delusion. We do, however, I suspect, go on thinking that the interaction between feminist text and reader is part of a fundamentally progressive narrative of individual and social enlightenment. It is this assumption that this study seeks to put into question.

There are two reasons for this: first, I try to show here that our trust in the successful powers of resistance-creation of the instrumental text is part of the means by which, in the end, things stay the same. As the ensuing chapters unpick the received stories of books that made radical changes to social systems, to reveal another story of nothing much happening, the possibility emerges that there are negative consequences to optimistic readings. In other words, the impulse to read *The Women's Room* as a successful intervention renders feminist criticism complicit with the hegemonic forces it most seeks to contest. Second, I think we need to question our (Anglo-American) commitment to success. I want to suggest that we might learn as much about resistance from a text that fails as from one that is embraced, whether in the moment or retrospectively, as a triumph of subversion. Whose terms do we uphold, after all, when we celebrate success?

THE PROBLEM OF RESISTANCE

To ask what a politically engaged text can do to the history and the reader it confronts, and how and when it can do it, requires that one be able to locate resistance, at least imaginatively, a fundamental point of theoretical and political difficulty in feminist debate. Margaret Homans's illuminating analysis in "Her Very Own Howl" of what at the time were distinct "french feminist" and "anglo-american" schools of feminist criticism, the one holding language to be that within which the subject is constituted, the

other believing in language's expressive properties, its availability
to the subject as a tool for self-definition and hence liberation, is in
effect an analysis of a difference of position about where resistance
can be found and its availability to the reader on a conscious level.
And the terms of the distinction still cause difficulty: Do we resist
with language, or does resistance take place within symbolic structure? The encounter between feminism and postmodernism pivots
around the problem of agency, which in a feminist context is always also the problem of how to resist. Those who repudiate the
postmodern vision of fragmentary subjectivities extruded by discourse do so in the name of a continued need for the capacity for
action; but postmodern feminist theory itself reconstructs at least
a strategic subject position, in order that opposition should have a
place to stand.[18]

The paradox of resistance is that a feminist theory must be able
to envisage a position that is both culturally saturated and somehow distanced from that culture, a (dis)location expressed by de
Lauretis's formulation the "eccentric subject," who inhabits a point
of view "necessary to feminism at this time," but not itself in history. De Lauretis's feminist split subject, at once caught in the
amber of ideologically produced femininity and "outside" that
structure because aware, reduces resistance to an act of will—to
the process of thinking and knowing that must, to be effective or
possible at all, take place in "a conceptual and experiential space
carved out of the social field."[19] But the increasing influence of
postcolonial studies on feminist thought, as well as, from a different direction, politically and theoretically, the effect of identity politics, has both demanded and allowed some rematerialization of
the resisting subject by reconstructing the concept of identity as
a multifaceted accumulation of political, geographical, and ethnic
positionings. The cultural hybrid, exemplified by the postcolonial
subject, is always, in quite specific, material ways, as well as internally, both inside and outside culture at once. Likewise, identity
studies' effect on feminist criticism has been to dislodge the imaginary unity of gender, opening up oppositional relations both
within and between individual subjects.[20] Subjectivity remains a
privileged location of resistance, even as that privilege is under
siege because of the seeming fragility of identity, and because of its
increasingly apparent multiplicity; the individual body, as the site

of culture's expression and inscription, must also be where resistance takes on manifest form.

But the instrumental text—if it is to be politically active—has another potential location of resistance: the social. Any text must act, in the first instance, on an individual level. But how is any effect on one reader at a time to be translated into some more general social change? In liberal feminism, the assertion of a text's transformative power is linked with a binary opposition between the individual subject and social formations. Such a structure produces only individual solutions to social problems: in a liberal theory of social organization, where the social and the institutional are seen as one, individuals can only succeed by triumphing over what must be an essentially immovable, monolithic object, "society." The path of liberal feminism has thus necessarily been the path of assimilation: if there is one central structure, salvation lies in adjusting its boundaries and its lines of control so that one is relocated inside. Such an individualist theory of resistance can lead, as Elizabeth Wilson has said, to an "assumption that the celebration of individual success and . . . triumph over adversity must represent a political position that is unproblematically progressive from a feminist perspective."[21] In such a framework, social change is envisaged as the movement of a mass of individuals into a different relation with a central structure that has not itself altered. While categories may expand or flex to allow in the civil rights of different sets of subjects, the locus of power has not shifted, and the control over definition remains centralized and remote.

Global change, affecting those not personally on the move, depends, in this theory of opposition, on gradual change in the universal values of the public sphere: something not previously seen as injustice (female subordination in the family, say) becomes visible as such, and thus change occurs; the process works by way of the accumulation of a critical mass of public opinion. A difficulty for a reformist program that acknowledges that the values of a society might need adjustment, or that to change the lines of exclusion only relocates injustice, is that change is not automatically produced by an accumulation of voices. The expressive power of language depends for its consequences on both the location of its expression and how it is received. While a persistent, and politically successful, rhetoric within feminism has emphasized the silencing of the female voice, speech does not in and of itself guarantee a disruptive outcome. As the patient on the couch talks herself back into synchronicity with the social structure that defines her, so female expression can operate as outlet and outcome, rather than attack. As Lauren Berlant argues, noting that certain mainstream media (such as women's magazines) have long legitimized women's complaints about their position without oppositional result, "the female complaint allows the woman who wants to maintain her alignment with men to speak oppositionally but without fear for her position within the heterosexual economy— because the mode of her discourse concedes the intractability of the (phallocentric) conditions of the complaint's production . . . the patriarchal social context . . . hystericizes it for her."[22]

A possible location for a collective form of opposition, moving beyond the atomized individual, is the "counter-public sphere." Felski defines the feminist counter-public sphere in *Beyond Feminist Aesthetics,* in terms closely modeled on the original notion of the classic public sphere of bourgeois public debate, as "an oppositional discursive arena within the society of late capitalism, structured around an ideal of a communal gendered identity perceived to unite all its participants."[23] It is a formulation that both reflects the reality of oppositional social movements and marginal identities and seeks to construct such a reality. The "official" public sphere thus becomes a dominant mechanism that is open to challenge, rather than the only available social structure, from which departure is deviance. Nonhegemonic formations become capable of producing alternative self-definitions, values, and cultural products that reflect those values. This refiguration of the public sphere envisages overlapping circles: a counter-public sphere that defines gender, class, ethnic, and sexual identity(ies) that are other than that of the universal public sphere nonetheless operates within the "official" public sphere. It is possible now to imagine, however, that as a member of a counter-public sphere, a subject is distanced from the products and values of the public sphere to a certain extent. The counter-public sphere(s) is a site of identity formation and of cultural production, and is thus potentially a location from which feminist texts and their readers emerge, and within which an audience both exists for and is constituted by feminist texts.

Like Raymond Williams's "structures of feeling," which similarly are designed to encode alternative ways of being only intermittently or emergently available to view on a material or institutional level, the counter-public sphere is not necessarily a reality on the level of "lived experience," a location that marginal subjects would recognize or that, once entered, defines one as marginal and only as marginal.[24] Particularly in relation to a feminist counter-public sphere, a text and its audience can be perceived or located by different subjects as a counter or official public sphere production. Texts—and readers—may move from one sphere to another—for example, counter-public sphere texts may be taken up by mainstream publishers and commentators. The shift here is not merely one of production and distribution: the effect of a text, how it is read, can alter as its location changes. For example, Rita Mae Brown's *Rubyfruit Jungle*, (1973) first issued by the counter-public sphere publishers Daughters Inc., is now a mass market paperback, and has become a representative text of lesbian experience for a mainstream audience rather than for the original lesbian reading cohort. But despite its shifting quality as category, the counter-public sphere is useful as a way of conceptualizing a location of both production and reception, or a sense of individual or collective identity that is defined in opposition to the mainstream but is not defined only in opposition to it, having separable values and ways of being of its own.

While Felski's definition is one based on a singular oppositional location and a single imaginary identification, that of gender, counter-public spheres are experienced by marginal subjects as multiple and often in contradiction.[25] The counter-public sphere is both imaginary and real, both actual geographical location (a site of production, for example) and internal placement (the way an individual positions herself in relation to a text, for example). As a way of constructing resistance it thus both moves away from the problem of subjectivity and returns to it with a difference: the reader becomes visible as anchored within a variety of possible institutional frameworks, rather than floating in ideal space. However, the status of the counter-public sphere as potentially— simultaneously or sequentially—both an attitude of mind and a location of nonhegemonic institutions of production is indicative of both the range of oppositional gestures that may issue from it, and their slipperiness. At its least material, the counter-public sphere could be simply another way of describing the mind as the real battleground, in Hogeland's formulation of feminist utopianism. And the '90s counter-public sphere that is a marketing niche—

the Queer Shopping Network, for example—is material, but not in the same way as the '70s collective printshop.[26]

The kind of oppositional gesture a text makes will vary according to its institutional position, depending, for instance, on whether it is an address to and from the counter or official public sphere. Rather than simply produce a hierarchy of value that privileges certain gestures over others whatever the historical circumstances, I argue that a reading of resistant texts requires, first, a more contingent, historically-inflected approach. The significance of such an approach can be explicated by way of Chéla Sandoval's theory of "oppositional consciousness."[27] Sandoval suggests that rival feminist theories (for example, liberal or marxist) have both conceptual and, potentially, organizational similarities with various oppositional strategies taken on by liberation movements (for example, civil rights or separatism). As liberation movements have used whatever strategy expresses resistance to a reigning ideology, so Sandoval proposes that proponents of feminist theories might recognize that these can likewise be regarded, and used, as modes of opposition, provisional models of truth, discourses to be deployed tactically as ideological weapons against shifting currents of power. Theory then itself becomes another tactic, not just the framework that guides other forms of engagement. The still point around which Sandoval's theory of cultural engagement turns is thus opposition itself, rather than either the particular methodology of opposition or the kinds of social change projected. My reading puts such a model into use in the reading and use of texts, producing a literary narrative of a range of texts in which opposition is expressed differentially.

I am not aiming to produce a model for the oppositional text; this seems to me the temptation of such an enterprise, but one that should particularly be avoided, since it is fundamental to the methodology of this reading that no such model can be considered to exist. The theory of opposition toward which my readings tend is likewise one that is marked by transience of effect: there can be no canon of oppositional texts as such if the capacity to create resistance is momentary—a consequence of fleeting conjunctures of textual and historical circumstances.[28]

Second, I am proposing that, given the contingency of oppositional effect, feminist critics reconsider a reading habit that values texts by their success or failure in this register. The chapters that follow accordingly seek to model a reading method that explores the relation between the shifting conditions of a text's reception over time and the positionings of its various readers. This approach abandons the search for the holy grail of the oppositional text. What emerges instead is a theory of oppositional possibility as created, re-created, and dissipated in a shifting round of readings—and uses of reading. The question asked of a text might thus become not Is it (successfully) oppositional? but How is it oppositionality put to use, and by whom?

The texts I examine in the following chapters are polemical: their intention to protest at and change the world they confront is always more or less explicit. Although I concentrate primarily upon examples of contemporary American narrative in fiction and film, I begin with Mary Wollstonecraft because, as author of *A Vindication of the Rights of Woman* (1792), Wollstonecraft functions as precursor for twentieth-century liberal feminism, credited with disseminating key ideas about women's rights and capacities. Read from the present, that is, Wollstonecraft is a powerful icon of resistance. Her "alternative" lifestyle, as well as *Rights of Woman* and, since its republication in the 1970s, *The Wrongs of Woman* (1798), have all been hailed as models of personal and political activism. As my analysis shows, however, it is only possible to reconstruct Wollstonecraft as the successful feminist polemicist by abstracting her work from the context of its reception. Reread within that context, her texts, and Wollstonecraft *as* text, emerge as examples of the power of the public sphere to act upon the oppositional object, be it text or body as text. Wollstonecraft becomes, returned to history, not the paradigm of the hitherto silenced woman, voice lifted in struggle and self-expression, but the visible body as field of representation for the purposes of others: her voice becomes a means to repressive counter-voicing.

Between the anathematizing of Wollstonecraft at the end of the 1790s and second-wave American feminism, social and cultural conditions have been transformed by changes in the literary marketplace and the structure of the public sphere. Wollstonecraft's successors can expect an audience, even if it is that of the counter-public sphere; the creation of alternative sources of cultural production and reception would seem to enhance the oppositional capacities of the feminist text, achieving by this new positioning precisely the social influence that Wollstonecraft, for lack of such structures, could not command. However, study of the reception of second-wave texts indicates that works addressed to a wide audience and that must, therefore, operate within the formations of the official public sphere are vulnerable to the reading process that that sphere enacts. I argue in chapters 2 and 3 that Marilyn French's bestseller *The Women's Room* and the Hollywood film *The Accused* are examples of mainstream cultural interventions whose oppositional intentions are finally reappropriated, despite readings that have proclaimed their political effectiveness. Chapter 2 explores the ways in which *The Women's Room* is constructed as a counter-public sphere text by both official public sphere and retrospective feminist critical readings, operations that simultaneously inflate and delimit the novel's power to change the social system it addresses. Chapter 3 reads *The Accused* through the original rape case on which it is based, arguing that the film's attempt to redress a social injustice is crucially undermined by its drive to utilize filmic techniques that replicate the mechanisms it seeks to critique.

Chapter 4 addresses the political viability of counter-public sphere productions through a reading of two works by and about Audre Lorde: Lorde's quasi autobiographical *Zami: A New Spelling of My Name* (1982), and *A Litany for Survival* (1995), a documentary film about Lorde's life made with the subject's active participation over several years before her death. Lorde's position as icon parallels that of Wollstonecraft in that both work and body exemplify resistance for contemporary readers. *Zami* is both an account of and in itself an act of self-creation, and thus follows a structure similar to that of French's novel and Kaplan's film, that in which an individual subject comes to self-consciousness and reconstructs her identity in light of a sense of that identity's coerced production within ideology. *A Litany for Survival* both repeats that narrative and comments upon it: it records Lorde's own recognition of and responses to her iconographic status as oppositional figure; the triumphal nature of the consciousness-raising process is thus recreated and deconstructed in the film, a bifurcation of effect which offers a possible pathway for a disabused but active criticism of resistance. Whereas the mainstream feminist texts I discuss are vulnerable to appropriation and rereading by the official public sphere, an examination of Lorde's reception shows that a counter-public sphere text—one produced by and for a marginal constituency—is in danger of appropriation less by the official cultural gatekeepers than by feminist criticism. *Litany for Survival* can be understood, therefore, as a resistant response to feminist constructions of Lorde as icon.

Throughout, I seek to raise questions about the uses to which feminist criticism has put both these texts in particular and the idea of the instrumental text itself. Without denying the strategic usefulness of both the concept and particular texts at particular times, I try to point up the limits on what texts can do, and to whom. Finally, in the Afterword I seek to promote a discussion of the critical and pedagogical implications for feminism of a revised theory of a fragile, fallible, and contingent instrumental text.

1

Mary Wollstonecraft, or the
Politics of Being Read

The publication of *A Vindication of the Rights of Woman* in 1792 established Wollstonecraft's reputation as polemicist and philosopher. Following the earlier *Vindication of the Rights of Man* (1790) and building on Wollstonecraft's first productions on education, *Rights of Woman*, judging by the wealth of public and private responses to the text, found an attentive audience. Her *Letters from Sweden* (1796) were successful and well received. Why, then, would Wollstonecraft, who said of novels' educational properties "from reading novels some women of superior talents learned to despise them," have chosen a return to fiction for what turned out to be her last work, *Maria or The Wrongs of Woman*, published posthumously in 1798?[1] While Wollstonecraft's final text has been variously explained as mere autobiography, as a retreat from controversy, and as a capitulation to acceptable feminine ways of knowing, the novel in the 1790s is also readily interpretable as an act of political engagement.[2] Indeed, at a moment when the instrumentality of the form was under intense scrutiny, an argument can be made for writing fiction as at least as much a radical, jacobin move as any extension of *Rights of Woman* into its projected second volume would have been. A close examination of the conditions that governed Wollstonecraft's shift of genre, and of how her novel was legible in the shifting, contested public sphere of the late 1790s, can illuminate the perils and possibilities of a late-eighteenth-century feminist's attempt to seize the novel as an agent for political change. But this enquiry will also serve to raise questions about contemporary feminist interventions in public discourse, where the novel remains an apparently compelling vehicle for feminist polemic. What does the use of this discourse enable, through its presumption of address to an individual reader, its

26

status as vehicle of personal enlightenment, its capacity to reach a female readership? What is foreclosed by these structuring conditions of form and reception? How does the novel's focus on individual transformation translate to or engage with a vision of its effectiveness as a means to social change?

The picture I have just sketched of *Rights of Woman* as successful polemic needs some complication in light of the difficulties attending a female rationalist's participation in the 1790s public sphere. While Wollstonecraft is now celebrated as a foremother of liberal feminist thought, her ideas brought about no movement of like-minded contemporary women to the barricades comparable to the political organizing and debate called into being by the text with which Wollstonecraft's invites comparison, Thomas Paine's *The Rights of Man*. One reason for this is that *Rights of Woman* does not *propose* that women organize, debate, or protest—unable to envisage the possibility of female collective action, Wollstonecraft does not include a mass women's invasion of the public sphere as part of her program of reform. In fact, the evidence of the text suggests that female public presence of any sort, collective or individual, actual or rhetorical, is fraught with anxiety. This position is a response to the constraints of contemporary discourse: Joan Landes has documented the creation at the time of the French Revolution of an historically specific, gendered bourgeois public sphere, structured around the silencing and domestication of women, in which public speech becomes explicitly gendered as masculine, while nature and natural difference are used to legitimate both woman's inferior position and her enclosure within the family. The systematic exclusion of women from the process of both debate and legislative activity in France after 1793 is at once justified and occluded by the creation and reification of the category of "republican womanhood," whereby woman's domestic role is given a civic gloss: her exile from the public sphere is rewritten as an opportunity for indirect participation through her nurturing and education of patriots at home.[3]

Many recent critics have read Wollstonecraft as complicit in the silencing of public women and in the identification of male speech with truth and reason. But this view simplifies Wollstonecraft's complex and shifting relations to the language(s) she uses.[4] Wollstonecraft's awkward attempts to appropriate rational discourse mark a scene not of capitulation to male occupation of right language, but rather of resistance and contestation. Wollstonecraft both critiques "feminine" rhetoric when used for Burkean purposes, and makes use of it herself. She gives room to speech that departs from the rational—the unguarded but inspirational thought, for instance, which repeatedly brings fruitful disorder to her thought process. Wollstonecraft also enacts the problematic encounter between male and female speakers, giving her antagonists embodiment and hence fallibility, playing with her own capacity to construct herself in their image. Throughout *Rights of Woman*, she very self-consciously performs the public act of debate, arguing with her antagonists, ridiculing them, claiming not to understand their position—generally attempting to demonstrate her mastery of rhetoric. The text is marked by her uneasy relation to a shifting and unreliable audience: when she is not explicitly exhorting or cajoling a more or less hostile male interlocutor, she is lamenting the absence or inattention of her female one.[5] Yet to accept the doctrine of republican womanhood is to acknowledge the inappropriateness of her own position in the public sphere, to render marginal her own voice even as she asserts her right to be heard. All Wollstonecraft's internal critics are male, and the logic of her own position does not promote the construction of fellow female speakers. *Rights of Woman*, then, is the production of a lone voice, and one that cannot seek to bring other women into the arena; the process of change must go forward through the persuasion of male citizens, those whose right to act in the public sphere is already acknowledged. Wollstonecraft is not unaware of the double bind in an argument that legislates that her words should fall on no female ears, cause no debate between women. Typically, *Rights of Woman*'s explicit acknowledgement of the radical woman's inevitable dependence on her male colleague's benevolence if her ideas are to find an audience is also a plea for change in these conditions:

> I . . . would fain convince reasonable men of the importance of some of my remarks; and prevail on them to weigh dispassionately the whole tenor of my observations. I appeal to their understandings; and, as a fellow-creature, claim, in the name of my sex, some interest in their hearts. I entreat them to assist to emancipate their companion, to make her a *helpmeet* for them. Would men but generously snap our chains . . . (263), Wollstonecraft's italics.

In the early 1790s, the possibility of that benevolence still carried some credibility. When Wollstonecraft suggests, in the dedication to Talleyrand that opens *Rights of Woman*, that rights for women have heretofore been neglected due only to an oversight that, once rendered visible, will soon be corrected, it is possible to believe that this is not merely a rhetorical gesture, but that she has some faith in public debate as a means to influence political and legislative decisions. But by 1796, when the project that became *Wrongs of Woman* was first proposed, it is hard to imagine that Wollstonecraft would harbor such expectations: the treason trials and the Gagging Acts, legal manifestations of the anti-jacobin sentiment by this time being institutionally promoted, were powerful indicators that the consequences of radical public speech were likely to be at least judicial harassment and censorship. The optimism of the early years of the Revolution, and the wide-ranging, relatively free debate that political change initiated in England, allowed Wollstonecraft in 1792 to both elide and to some extent negotiate the exclusion of women from the public sphere, the consequent lack of a female audience of like minds, and the anomalousness of her own rhetorical position; but a change in the political climate brings these structural difficulties into sharper focus. Circumstances allowed Wollstonecraft to equivocate in *Rights of Woman* as to the necessity for her purpose of the existence of female readers. In 1796 it might well seem that the novel is the only place to go in search of an audience of any kind.

One of Wollstonecraft's biographers, Eleanor Flexner, suggests that it was the new caution brought about by her pregnancy in 1796 that led Wollstonecraft to turn to "uncontroversial subjects for her writing—literature, the care of children, and another novel."[6] Flexner's comment emerges out of a modern cultural structure that assumes a naturalized division between politics and art, a boundary that art crosses only to its detriment and at risk of becoming other than itself. Whatever the effect of hormonal changes upon Wollstonecraft's thought processes, however, no contemporary of hers could or would assume that the writing of a novel would place its author beyond reach of political controversy. Flexner's position reflects the result of a battle over the cultural positioning and form of the novel that was still being fiercely contested in the 1790s. Conservative forces would unequivocally estab-

lish the novel as a noninstrumental genre during the first decades
of the nineteenth century, but when Wollstonecraft began *Wrongs*
jacobins and anti-jacobins alike saw fiction as a mode of discourse
that both necessarily partook of its author's political beliefs and
operated to inculcate its readers with those beliefs.

This is why discussions of the instrumentality of novels, usually
couched in terms of their deleterious effect on impressionable
young women, are routine throughout the eighteenth century.
Wollstonecraft's own book reviews for the *Analytical Review* are typical in identifying novel-reading with moral degeneracy: "a great
number of pernicious and frivolous novels are daily published,
which only serve to heat and corrupt the minds of young women,
and plunge them . . . into that continual dissipation of thought
which renders all serious employment irksome."[7] Writers de-
fended their work not by claiming it as noninstrumental but as
exceptional to the general rule of bad influence, as Fanny Burney
does in her Preface to *Evelina*; because she has been true, as writers
of "Romance" have not, to Reason and Nature, her book may be
read "if not with advantage, at least without injury."[8] The anti-
jacobin Jane West's declaration in *A Gossip's Story* (1796), a novel
going through its third edition in 1798, seems, at first glance, consistent with the traditional claim to be the exceptional novel that
builds moral fiber. But the stock intention "to illustrate the Advantages of Consistency, Fortitude, and the Domestic Virtues; and to
expose to ridicule, Caprice, Affected Sensibility, and an Idle Cen-
sorious Humour," is, it turns out, to be employed as the antidote
to that "poison" which "enemies of our church and state continue
to pour . . . into unwary ears through this channel."[9] West's starkly
politicized view of her purpose illustrates the extent to which the
domestic sphere has become the field not merely of moral battle
but of political strife, and the novel a likely conduit for seditious
ideas.

The intense politicization of the novel in the 1790s is a logical
and inevitable consequence of the politicization of the domestic
sphere. Edumund Burke's production of the family as the first
ground of patriotism in *Reflections on the Revolution in France*
(1790)—the place, by extension, where the war against a French
Revolution in England and against France itself would be won or
lost—led to the family's reading matter becoming potentially the
troubling site of political influence.

For radicals, the jacobin novel briefly seemed a means whereby their revolutionary ideas could be conveyed in peaceful, domesticated terms. The heroines of jacobin novels, like their predecessors, suffer under tyrannical fathers and faithless lovers, but new rules govern their behavior. In the jacobin novel of the 1790s— Robert Bage's *Hermsprong* or Thomas Holcroft's *Anna St. Ives*, for example—disobedience to paternal authority is canvassed by protagonists as a legitimate principle of conduct. Girls know better than their fathers, not because, like Clarissa, they are closer to God but because their education and subsequent experience have brought them to political enlightenment.[10]

The conditions that legitimated the use of the novel as radical instrument were under some pressure by 1796. As the perceived threat of invasion from without or insurrection from within escalated, it was the anti-jacobin novel that came to dominate in the field of instrumental fiction, reaching a peak of production in 1799–1800. *Wrongs* is probably the last jacobin novel published, if not the last written.[11] But in 1796, while the genre still seemed open to appropriation, Wollstonecraft could view the embattled form as offering the advantages of a polemic as forum for exploration of controversial ideas, without either the problems of address she encountered in *Rights of Woman* or the immediate danger of prosecution for sedition.

Because *Wrongs* has often been read as a retreat from the political arena, it is worth emphasizing that the novel does require reading as an instrumental, jacobin text, however compelling its other claims to meaning within competing modes of discourse such as sensibility.[12] Wollstonecraft's Preface positions her unequivocally within the arena of political debate. She declares as her "main object . . . the desire of exhibiting the misery and oppression, peculiar to women, that arise out of the partial laws and customs of society."[13] Her comments in a letter to George Dyson, extracted by Godwin and reproduced after the Preface, give further credence to an activist conception of the novel. Indeed, this outline of her plans, taken together with the Preface's stipulation that "the history ought rather to be considered, as of woman, than of an individual" (73), seems to line up the novel very closely with the project of the *Rights of Woman*:

These appear to me (matrimonial despotism of heart and conduct) to be the peculiar Wrongs of Woman, because they degrade the mind. . . .

> This is what I have in view; and to show the wrongs of different classes
> of women, equally oppressive, though, from the difference of educa-
> tion, necessarily various. (74)

Of course, the Preface's relation to the work it frames is by no
means either obvious or unitary, not least because this is a publication prepared by Godwin after Wollstonecraft's death. The Preface
allows the reader to anticipate a companion text to *Caleb Williams*
(1794), whose purpose Godwin defines in that work's Preface as "a
general review of the modes of domestic and unrecorded despotism, by which man becomes the destroyer of man."[14] But the
opening paragraph of Wollstonecraft's text, by invoking the vocab-
ulary of sensibility and, by strong association, the female reader of
that text, at once opens a gap between this work and Godwin's.
Can Wollstonecraft reach Godwin's reader with her text? Does she
seek to do so? And how can the female reader she seems to call up
also operate as a politicized reader? I think that *Wrongs* is an attempt to reimagine into being a forum of free debate. Wollstonecraft solves the problem of her own lack or failure of agency in the
public sphere—her sense that even the imperfect forum available
to the earlier *Vindications* is no longer open to her—by restaging
the public sphere debate about the "wrongs of woman" in the
space still available to her, that of the narrative of *Wrongs of Woman*.

Wollstonecraft's dilemma as a feminist polemicist without either
a defined audience or a secure form with which to reach that audience finds both expression and solution in the novel's full title: *The
Wrongs of Woman: Or, Maria. A Fragment. The Wrongs of Woman*, as I
have been suggesting, invokes both *Rights of Woman* and *Rights of
Man*; it announces itself a polemic that will address woman in the
abstract, woman as sociological study and legal entity. One expects
a rhetorical method of argumentation of such a document, the
rational discourse of public sphere debate. Placing itself in the
niche that Wollstonecraft and others have already carved for such
philosophical discussions, it also claims to go beyond precursors
and models, covering the antithetical and apparently new ground
of "wrongs." *Maria*, on the other hand, invokes fictional narratives
of female sensibility, referring back to a host of heroines of the
proliferating contemporary novel as well as to Wollstonecraft's own
early production, *Mary* (1788). The definition through first name

invites us to expect intimacy of address, the private thoughts of the individual produced in the mode of sentiment.

These two parts are brought into connection by "Or." The little conjunction sits quietly on the page, defying the difficulties that seem to lie on either side of it, proclaiming the equivalence of these two texts: the private story of Maria is the same as The Wrongs of Woman. This is genre-formation at its most condensed. The personal is political; the jacobin novel is the novel of sensibility. What the title can assert, however, the text itself cannot necessarily deliver. The problem of the text, indeed, lies in the establishment and maintenance of that equivalence, or at least in the workings out of its possibilities. How is the personal narrative, the fictive sentimental text, to become a presence in the public sphere, an indictment carrying authority in the arena of rational debate?

There is a third part of the title, "A Fragment," and this marks both text and title as editorial rather than authorial creations. Had Wollstonecraft lived, Godwin would not have published a fragmented, unfinished manuscript; and perhaps, too, the title of a work controlled by Wollstonecraft would not have echoed so directly Godwin's *Things As They Are; or, The Adventures of Caleb Williams*. Yet, Wollstonecraft's or not, the title points to a crucial difficulty with which author and text must tangle; insofar as it is useful or possible to distinguish between the text and its apparatus as author might have intended it and editor produced it, the most that can be said is that Godwin's framing draws particular attention to Wollstonecraft's struggle with the conventions and possibilities of the novel at a destabilized historical moment.

The novel itself enacts the reception of the sentimental text in the public sphere, modeling how such a document should be received, narrating the process of enlightenment and change that can follow. But at the same time as Wollstonecraft narrates a scene of successful feminist agency, she also depicts the myriad misreadings that can befall such a text, and the seemingly infinite capacities of narrative to ensnare both writer and reader. Although *Wrongs* announces itself as showing the reader that writing and reading *can* constitute action, much of the text demonstrates a dichotomous relationship between narrative and agency: to write or read is almost by definition not to act.

Wollstonecraft's Preface presents the novel as illustrative of juridical injustice, and in line with this theme, the plot of the novel

shows that the law acts to entrap rather than protect the female
subject: any attempt to escape a violent, abusive husband is interpreted as a failure of female submissiveness. On this level, the story
is that of the citizen asserting, and failing to secure, her rights in
the public sphere. Thus *Wrongs* opens with the heroine imprisoned in an asylum by her husband, who has also kidnapped their
infant daughter and intends by these stratagems to ensure that
Maria's inheritance reverts to him. Maria is befriended in the mad-
house by her female gaoler, Jemima, and by another unjustly imprisoned inmate, Darnforth, with whom Maria falls in love.
Escaping, Maria is deserted by the fickle Darnforth, denied her
daughter, a divorce and her fortune in court, and (in the most
extended of several fragmentary alternative endings) is dissuaded
from suicide only by the reappearance of Jemima and the lost infant. The bulk of the narrative is taken up with extensive flash-
backs and personal narratives on the part of the main protagonists,
each of whom tells their life histories, either to each other or, in
Maria's case, as a document to be passed down to her daughter.

In the court scene, Wollstonecraft sets out the feminist night-
mare—the lone woman crying for justice within an institution
where her voice can never be heard. Pleading for her right to love
another since her husband has abused her, for the right to a divorce and the return of her property, Maria is rejected by the
judge on overtly political grounds, "We did not want French principles in public or private life" (199), and also because of the sentimental (private sphere) basis of her appeal: "[T]he judge, in
summing up the evidence, alluded to 'the fallacy of letting women
plead their feelings, as an excuse for the violation of the marriage-
vow' " (198). As Tillotama Rajan has pointed out, the horror of this
scene is a transparent invitation to the reader to invert the plot in
her mind, restoring to Maria the power to act. As well as restoring
Maria to agency, we are encouraged to reread Maria's actions
through the gauze of *Rights of Woman*, arriving thus at a sense of
the limitations of Maria's political awareness.[15] Rajan illustrates
through this episode in the text the liberating or "divinatory"
reading that she persuasively argues Wollstonecraft requires:
meaning is not inherent in the text but rather is produced and
reproduced by the creative, historicizing, and historicized reader.
In these successive, fleeting resolutions of the text by the activist
reader, Maria's trapped passivity is both repudiated and resolved.

My reservation about this very compelling explication of Wollstonecraft's text and hermeneutic methodology is that it seems to
solve the one problem that the text wants to depict as beyond solv-
ing: by heroizing the Romantic reader who, outside the text and
with the benefit both of *Rights of Woman* and of hindsight, is able to
put the pain of women's wrongs to rest, Rajan comes close to allowing the reader into the very position of transcendence that both
her own and Wollstonecraft's critical operations are designed to
problematize. It is the project of *Wrongs* to ensure that the reader
of a narrative is always both suspect (because likely to be distorting
what she reads) and entrapped (by the power of the narrative itself). While Rajan relies on the self-reflexive reader to question
her own transcendence, Wollstonecraft's text reaches for solutions
outside the enclosure of the individual's encounter with that text.
Rather than seek for the perfect reader, Wollstonecraft tries instead to create a different place of reading—a place that is constructed by no individual reader, reading, but by another context,
a differently constituted public sphere.

The communication—specifically, the impossibility of communication—between the judge and Maria reproduces the fate of the
sentimental text in an unreconstructed public sphere, where the
female speaker, by virtue of both gendered body and mode of discourse, has neither voice nor audience. Rather than leave the creation of a sympathetic audience to posterity, as Rajan would have
it, Wollstonecraft models that audience, and the kind of public
sphere in which individual histories can be politically active, within
the text of *Wrongs*. Literally imprisoned, and further caged by a
system of laws that curtail their freedom of movement and action,
Maria and Darnforth convey ideas to each other and the world
through narrative; they and Jemima form each other's audience.
This cycle of interpretation and reinterpretation, preconception
and misconception, establishes the generative power of narrative.
Maria's account of her own life is both a document in private circu-
lation—read by Darnforth, it is instrumental in their growing intimacy—and a public text, the history she sets out for the education
of her daughter. Because the daughter is part of an imaginary
future, however, she stands in the same relation to Maria's life
story as does the putative reader of *Wrongs* to the completed text—
the novel cannot enact its own reception, nor can Maria rest in the
certainty that her diary will work upon her daughter's mind as

she wishes. All these stories demonstrate a vast potential for effects without presenting an ideal model for reading. Only when Jemima tells her story do text and reception coexist within the text, enabling the production of a model of public opinion formation.

The events Jemima recounts are those of many a sentimental tale—seduction, ruin, abandonment. But this individual history is also presented as proof of the systemic production of the degraded woman of *Rights*: Jemima is an oppressed working-class woman whose life is determined by the social structures that created her and her environment. Her narrative asks to be read as polemic, without relinquishing the mechanisms that operate within the sentimental individual history. Both Maria and Darnforth, listening, recognize that they are hearing, in Wollstonecraft's words, a "history [that] ought rather to be considered, as of woman, than of an individual." Darnforth's response acknowledges that, contrary to contemporary ideology, the poor are usually rendered miserable by poverty, while Maria urges Jemima on with the assurance that she does not speak without effect: "your narrative gives rise to the most painful reflections on the present state of society" (115). Later, reflecting on what she has heard, Maria realizes that this history is generalizable in relation to gender as well as class: "[T]hinking of Jemima's peculiar fate and her own, she was led to consider the oppressed state of women" (120).

The reception accorded Jemima's narrative is surely that which Wollstonecraft wishes to engender for *Wrongs* itself; it serves as a model for readers both in and outside the text for how opinion can legitimately be formed by the history of an individual that refers persuasively to general truths. Here sentiment is no barrier to rational understanding and opinion-formation, but rather its essential vehicle. However, the model is no sooner in place than the text works to undermine its efficacy. Having shown Jemima's narrative as active agent, *Wrongs* then seems compelled to point up the limitations of its power, the tendency of that power to turn upon itself.

The production of Jemima's story itself marks a stage in Jemima's own sentimental education. Initially suspicious of Maria, and given only to "exclamations and dry remarks," she is gradually led to the river of sensibility both by association with Maria's emotions and by the sentimental communion she observes between Maria and Darnforth. Only when her receptivity to emotion is assured is Jemima able to enter the flow of narration; the capacity to produce the private history that will operate appropriately in the public sphere depends upon access to, and use of, sentiment. Her new power is that capacity to act upon others; but sensibility is also susceptibility *to* others. The full account of Maria's reception of Jemima's story, quoted in part above, goes beyond Maria's political enlightenment—in fact, Maria shifts immediately back from political to personal: ". . . she was led to consider the oppressed state of women, and to lament that she had given birth to a daughter" (120). Brought by Jemima's cautionary tale to an awareness of her own infant's danger, Maria realizes that the newly sentimentalized Jemima can be the means to the child's rescue. She reworks Jemima's own story in order to persuade her to act on the child's behalf, cementing the return to the personal through the creation of an imaginary domestic relation. Jemima's reward will be a retreat to the delights of surrogate motherhood in the private sphere ("I will teach her to consider you her second mother" [121]). With macabre skill, Maria converts a narrative that had seemed to be entitled "The Wrongs of a Class of Women" into "Jemima" and uses it upon the author, who now "ha[s] not the power to resist this persuasive torrent" (121).

Wrongs problematizes its own program for the genre, as if to suggest that the sentimental novel as agent of change in the public sphere is not an idea that Wollstonecraft can sustain beyond the scandal of its momentary imagining. It is perhaps no accident that the turn from social to individual is also a return of the working-class woman to the position of succorer of the middle class. In part this conceptual withdrawal can also be linked back to Wollstonecraft's gendered assumptions about how action is organized in the public sphere, and by whom. Jemima's story works upon Maria, and while both parties to the communication recognize the location of that encounter as the public sphere of abstract discourse, as women they are collectively impaired, and can be imagined as capable only of individual action, or of action on behalf of the family: both Maria and Jemima have therefore to be remotivated by personal considerations before either can act, Maria in persuading Jemima, Jemima in searching for the lost child. Wollstonecraft's return from public to private can also be read as another, and perhaps the most far-reaching, instance of the text's production of narrative as containment. The thematic of imprisonment works itself out both through and in narrative: *Wrongs* is the story of a woman's imprisonment, but it is also a woman's imprisonment in story. Even when the text most successfully produces narrative as positive force in the public sphere, it must reenact a hermeneutic of suspicion, the fear that any public text can be read back into the private.

In *Wrongs*, narrative is always communication and miscommunication, source of truth and source of misrepresentation. While layers of narrative seem to proliferate endlessly as the characters circulate their own life histories, their novels, the marginal notations on those novels, and the images of each other which reading the novels calls forth, the direction of misreading, at least, is consistent. Reading Darnforth's books, hearing his personal narrative, imagining him through the lens of Rousseau, Maria is always in danger of sentimental delusion and paralysis. Writing her own story, she finds that she has "buried [herself] alive"; the descent into the text of sentiment is a move away from the possibility of or desire for action. Yet writing and reading are always also the only means the prisonhouse offers of knowing. Rajan suggests that the only escape from this tightly wound circle is provided by the reader outside the text, she who, even while enmeshed in her own partial misreading, can escape from the delusions that threaten to drown Maria, the sentimental subject, who will die smiling, convinced that the ocean of passivity in which she floats is a sea of hope criss-crossed by manly knights sailing to her rescue. But Maria, too, is an active reader. Wollstonecraft's binary opposition between reading and action breaks down exactly because of the novel's reflexive awareness of the power of narrative: in the novel itself, reading *is* action, although it is only action in the space available, the private sphere.

The active reading that Maria performs is, often, a means to self-delusion. Darnforth is not—in any of the tentative endings provided by Godwin or according to such hints as the more finished parts of the copy offer—the savior and soul mate she constructs for herself. The narrator excuses Maria for this weakness—she is, after all, only what her environment has made her: "what chance then had Maria of escaping, when pity, sorrow, and solitude all conspired to soften her mind, and nourish romantic wishes, and, from a natural progress, romantic expectations?" (98). But this passionate revision of Darnforth cannot simply be dismissed as misreading, for Maria's fall into romance is also an occasion of active, creative manipulation of her environment:

> Besides, what are we, when the mind has, from reflection, a certain kind of elevation, which exalts the contemplation above the little concerns of prudence! We see what we wish, and make a world of our own—and, though reality may sometimes open a door to misery, yet the moments of happiness procured by the imagination, may, without a paradox, be reckoned among the solid comforts of life. Maria now, imagining that she had found a being of celestial mould—was happy—nor was she deceived—He was then plastic in her impassioned hand—and reflected all the sentiments which animated and warmed her. (188–89)

Maria's work here has been to provide an individual solution for a social problem: unable to alter the conditions of legal disenfranchisement in which she finds herself, she makes Darnforth into the protective paragon of romantic endings. Because this is not simply *Maria* but also *The Wrongs of Woman*, her fiction is not sustainable or credible—the novel ends elsewhere, whether in suicide or in rescue, always without benefit of the masculine hero. The text thus enacts both the power and the insufficiency of the unilaterally privatized, individual solution-producing narrative. In playing out Maria's attempt to write herself a love story, the narrative puts the two halves of its title into jarring dissonance: the *Wrongs of Woman* cannot be solved by the generic imaginings of the romantic *Maria*. The connection between the two parts is politicized; its grammatical possibilities proliferate: *Maria* becomes visible as the ideological cover for Wrongs, that which would disguise it through seductive misrepresentation; *Maria* can now be seen as a post facto, incommensurate, but necessary extrusion of Wrongs—because Wrongs, therefore *Maria*. *Maria*, the delusory romance, is motivated by the Wrongs of woman: the place of the woman in the private sphere is a response—dishonest, delusory and insufficient, whatever its satisfactions—to her absence, her Wrongedness, in the public sphere.

The title of a text is its theory, the body its praxis. The full title of Wollstonecraft's work proposes an available relationship between personal and political, private and public spheres: the sentimental novel can achieve meaning and agency as part of a free exchange in the arena where opinion is formed and changed. In the working out of this proposition that is the text, the theory of the sentimental narrative's being active in the public sphere is tested and proves untenable. The titular "Or" becomes ideologically charged, and the relationship between the two discourses on either side is revealed as one of struggle. The body of the text enacts the failure of its theory, rendering visible the consequences of the attempt to speak the female text in the theater of rationality. A text that claims to be active in a public sphere debate shows that that debate cannot take place.

The dynamic could be described in terms of a utopian title presiding over a dystopian text, the "ought" of the title standing against the "is" of the text. Both these formulations allow a reading of *Wrongs* as not naively but *knowledgeably* enacting its failure. In the present of the actual public sphere, Jemima the feminist speaker goes unheard, while Maria the sentimentalized domestic woman internalizes her oppression. But Wollstonecraft's fragmented text also imagines into being another public sphere, not of the future but of *the alternative present*, one in which *Maria* is understood to speak eloquently and instrumentally of the Wrongs of Woman; here are not new readers but rather a new framework within which to read.

Wollstonecraft died without completing *Wrongs*, so we cannot know that it would ever have been finished had Wollstonecraft survived childbirth, still less what form the novel might finally have taken. Wollstonecraft's death also dictated that the form of the text that was published be a construction of Godwin's, framed by his introductory cautions and apologies. The history of the reading of *Wrongs* is not of a reception defined by a fragmentary, incomplete text, however. In the immediate, *Wrongs* was not read because Godwin's *Memoirs of the Author of A Vindication of the Rights of Woman* (1798) were, setting off a chorus of condemnation.

In the *Memoirs* Godwin sets out unequivocally the circumstances of Wollstonecraft's life, scandalous and otherwise, including the details of her affair with Gilbert Imlay and the birth of their illegitimate daughter, Wollstonecraft's suicide attempts, and the details of Godwin's own affair with Wollstonecraft prior to their marriage. Godwin's motivation for these revelations is usually taken to be a kind of bumbling naivete about the shock value of Wollstonecraft's history: the absent-minded philosopher, further muddied by grief, is out of touch with the real world that gossips outside his ivory tower. In fact, Godwin is consistent and purposeful. It is apparent from the organization of the text that part of his motivation in publishing the *Memoirs* is the opportunity that memorializing Wollstonecraft provides for justifying and reiterating his own beliefs; hence, for example, the statement "We did not marry" is immediately followed by his lengthy disquisition on the irrelevance of ceremony to sanctify passion, and only belatedly, in what seems like an afterthought, by an account of Wollstonecraft's own position. Her life becomes an illustration of his principles in action.[16]

It is also true that, as twentieth-century critics have pointed out, Godwin's account of Wollstonecraft, and in particular his rendition of their relationship, relies on gender stereotypes: they are complementary, she providing the intuitive qualities that supplied Godwin's own lack in this respect. But at the same time as Godwin emphasizes Wollstonecraft's feminine sensibility, appealing to the reader to sympathize and admire her as a "female Werther," she is nonetheless rendered as a hero. Godwin sees Wollstonecraft's death as having freed her from the need to compromise with the contingent mores of her social milieu and its transient values. The fact of death renders possible a standard of judgment that is universal:

> There are no circumstances of her life, that, in the judgment of honor and reason, could brand her with disgrace. Never did there exist a human being, that needed, with less fear, expose all their actions, and call upon the universe to judge them. An event of the most deplorable sort, has awfully imposed silence upon the gabble of frivolity.[17]

She is produced as a public figure, one who lays claim to the status of model citizen. It is this attempted insertion of the exemplary female body into masculine discursive space that, it seems to me, accounts for the public reaction to Godwin's candor, for his revelations are aimed not merely at suggesting a new truth for the domestic sphere (where passion should not be made to wait upon ceremony), but at making Wollstonecraft a civic model for anyone to follow.[18]

Godwin's project in *Memoirs* is disruptive of boundaries between public and private. He deprivatizes Wollstonecraft's life, but he is also rewriting the sentimental text—seduction, abandonment, attempted suicide—the text of *Maria*, as it might be transformed through a different generic convention or reading possibility: in the *Memoirs* Wollstonecraft's life becomes a kind of jacobin novel, an exemplary *bildung* to political enlightenment. Godwin's act, while always read as revealing what is too private, is in fact enforced against because it is too public.

However, Wollstonecraft's life becomes, in its reception, emphatically a privatized text; the exemplary, public discourse is transformed into one of individual pathology. In effect, Godwin's creation of Wollstonecraft as immortal paragon, disembodied signifier of virtue, calls forth its other: the fallible Wollstonecraft body as proof both of bad doctrine and of the absence of doctrine. The reconversion from public to private, abstract to actual, is performed with exceptional, clarifying fervor by Richard Polwhele, for whom Wollstonecraft's life and death become a parable of freedom from restraint, upon which excess is visited the ultimate confinement:

> [T]he Hand of Providence is visible, in her life, her death, and the Memoirs themselves. As she was given up to her "heart's lust," and let "to follow her own imaginations," that the fallacy of her doctrines . . . might be manifested to the world; and as she died a death that strongly marked the distinction of the sexes, by pointing out the destiny of women, and the diseases to which they are liable; so her husband was permitted, in writing her Memoirs, to labour under a temporary infatuation, that every "incident might be seen without a gloss—every fact exposed without an apology."[19]

For Polwhele, all female discourse providentially collapses into contingent physicality, the fallibility of female speech divinely inscribed in the decaying flesh of death in childbirth. The body is revealed as the source of what once appeared to be ideas but are now visible as physical emissions of the inexorably corporeal female self, that which public discourse seeks to control. While Polwhele typifies the extreme of conservative reaction, even sympathetic critics respond by reading Wollstonecraft out of the public sphere into the safety of the domestic, reanalyzing abstract argument as personal complaint. As the *Monthly Visitor*'s reviewer has it, "But indeed she was no modern philosopher. . . . And, in all probability, had she been married well in early life, she had then been a happy woman, and universally respected."[20] With terrifying, vertiginous compactness, all of Wollstonecraft's narrations collapse into one another, becoming legible only as the story of a private life. In an eerie duplication of the failures of reading in *Wrongs*, the novel itself is erased, as polemic and even as fiction, emerging in contemporary accounts only as a reprision of Wollstonecraft's own experience. Just as Jemima's story and Maria's petition to the court—generalizing narratives about systemic oppression—become in their reception only privatized accounts of feeling, so does *Wrongs* become Wollstonecraft's *apologia pro vita sua:* "Whoever shall compare [*Wrongs*] with the life of Mrs. Godwin, must perceive that it is also designed as vindication of her own opinions and conduct."[21]

Between the publication of Godwin's *Memoirs* in 1798 and a reprint of *The Wrongs of Woman* in 1976, Wollstonecraft's last novel seems literally to have gone unread. The only exceptions to this are Wollstonecraft's successive biographers, who continue the tradition of reading *Wrongs* as autobiography, and as such generically neither fiction nor polemic: "she had no creative gift and this so-called fiction is but a medley composed of Mary's own experiences"; "she found it hard to resist the opportunity for describing aspects of her childhood once again."[22] As catalyst of social change, *Wrongs* would on this showing seem to have been completely unsuccessful, this last and most enduring generic revision ensuring that this is a text that speaks only in the most privatized terms.

Wollstonecraft did not, however, vanish completely as a presence in the public sphere: she lingers on as handy anathema, a bogeywoman called up frequently to frighten the girls.[23] The spate of anti-jacobin material that, while reaching its height in terms of both quantity and virulence at the turn of the century, continued to dominate into the second decade of the 1800s included a persistent thread of reference to Wollstonecraft. In periodicals she appears as the standard invidious comparison, source of philosophical and social contagion, guaranteeing by association the danger of other women's ideas: "Mrs. Randall avows herself of the school of Wollstoncroft [*sic*]; and that is enough for all who have any regard to decency, order, or prudence, to avoid her company."[24]

In novels of the period, a Wollstonecraftian woman embodies

the dire consequences of free love or radical thinking; as she languishes, abandoned by her lover, or makes herself ridiculous by cross-dressing and fighting duels, she serves as a constant reminder of the dangers of woman's emergence from domestic protection. An instructive example of Wollstonecraft's half-life as negative exemplum occurs in the December 1799 issue of the periodical *Lady's Monthly Museum*—obviously addressed to a female audience, this magazine signals its intention to provide suitable models for feminine accomplishment through long, adulatory biographies of contemporary women writers. In a letter purporting to be written by an anguished mother whose daughters had been radically altered by reading Wollstonecraft's *Rights of Woman*, readers are given an extended description of the alleged effect of Wollstonecraft's corrosive words on the sanctity of the domestic sphere. The young women are taught by *Rights of Woman* to seek masculine pleasures, debased forms of economic exchange, and display: they gamble, race horses, duel, and debate radical ideas with unruly mobs. In all these scenes, the female body is depicted as horribly revealed by the girls' move from private to public space. One daughter, however, performs her operations at home:

> Clara, the third, distresses me by her cruelty. She studies anatomy; and one evening, disguised in a suit of boy's cloaths, went to a Lecture on that horrid subject. Since which, she thinks she herself is able to dissect; and I now cannot keep dog or cat alive in the house. About a month ago, she enticed a monkey (which was a present from an only brother who is abroad) into her room. This brute she killed, and dissected, before any one knew what was become of him. Since that she has had two corpses from the Resurrection men. The skeletons of these are placed on different sides of her room, facing each other. I would describe the room to you, but that it is too shocking a subject to dwell upon; but it is likest to a slaughter-house of any thing that I know of.[25]

Here is the ultimate threat—instead of Wollstonecraft as the petticoated hyena that wanders the public discursive streets seeking whom it may devour, we have the hyena within doors, polluting the most intimate reaches of the family home. The literalized devouring woman, her boudoir a slaughterhouse, forcefully embodies the dangers of masculine knowledge in feminine hands, masculine philosophical discourse in Wollstonecraft's mouth. *Rights* has become almost a novel here in its capacity to enter the domestic fastness, in its capacity to seduce and demoralize. The letter specifies that the antidote to such danger is the enactment of its actual consequences as rendered visible on the bodies and homes of its victims:

> Such, Sir, is the history of my family; and such as it is I lay it before the public, to warn all those young women who may feel inclined to favour the new philosophy. In my family they may see it in practice.[26]

It is in practice, in the flesh, that Wollstonecraft is most demonstrably absurd and abhorrent; in theory, the letter writer hints, there is a dangerous persuasiveness to her words.

The simulacra of Wollstonecraft that inhabit a public sphere closed, after 1798, to her own words function in part to neutralize her ideas by rendering them ridiculous. They also serve to create the impression that Wollstonecraft has not been silenced: ventriloquized by conservative puppet-masters, she seems still to figure on the public stage, creating a kind of virtual free debate in which the process of opinion formation is already fixed. Finally, the images of Wollstonecraft are images not only of monstrosity, of Polwhele's unsexed females, but also of power. As terrifying grotesque, Wollstonecraft the hyena is a force against which an increasingly controlled, univocal public sphere can legitimately arm itself. Wollstonecraft is used, that is, as a policing fantasy, the fantasy of oppositional violence that allows into being a controlling regime.

Habermas's "literary public sphere," the space where women and others excluded from the official public sphere may enjoy a kind of participation in debate through reading literature, is glossed by Anne Mellor as in fact amounting in the 1790s to a feminist counter-public sphere. Given an increasing female audience, and a growing body of women writing for that audience, Mellor claims reading as "potentially a feminist act," an oppositional search for knowledge officially denied women, and novels as a counter-public sphere "designed to educate female public opinion."[27] But the reception of *Wrongs* clarifies the extent to which the conditions for addressing a female audience, for entering into a debate on women's issues, did not exist by the end of the 1790s. The mere existence of a body of potential readers is not enough in itself to constitute a counter-public sphere. Wollstonecraft's shift into the novel form, then, is an insufficient condition for polemical agency, given that the structuring conditions of production and reception are those of a hostile official public sphere, and that no alternative site exists.

Nonetheless, Wollstonecraft's choice of the novel suggests an attempt to create that absent alternative—and I have been arguing that the novel form enables her to model the workings of a counter-public sphere as the polemic debating structure of *Rights of Woman* does not. In the created world of the novel, she can imagine into being her own sympathetic audience, and thus the process whereby public opinion is influenced. So while Wollstonecraft's novel can tell us little about the actual instrumental possibilities of fiction as it works upon either the individual reader or the social structure within which she reads, it is useful as a possible model for what the feminist novel in general thinks it does, and how. A generation of feminist writers in the 1970s perceived their relation to the public sphere as as embattled and hostile as was Wollstonecraft's, and the belief in fiction as a potentially effective weapon may be based on similar constructions of the novel reader as a sympathetic and impressionable listener. It remains to be seen whether the contemporary formation of counter-public spheres, their audiences and their means of production, are the sufficient conditions to enable fiction to create social change.

The representation of Wollstonecraft produced by the anti-jacobin public sphere is that of instrumental power barely contained, and it is this conception of Wollstonecraft that contemporary feminism inherited. She appears in the cultural imagination as an effective champion of women's rights; it is only on close examination that we realize that no social change can be attributed to her influence, that if anything her ideas have been used to justify repression. The idea of the feminist writer as a monster of enormous strength is an ideological production that continues to carry weight; even in the 1970s it will be seen to operate in the official sphere as threat to be enforced against, while contemporary feminist writers' belief in their own powers also seemed to be linked to that vision of disruptive energy. If Wollstonecraft is largely a negative model of the feminist novelist as agent of change, she is none the less an illuminating and instructive one, and no less relevant to the questions to be asked of contemporary feminist fiction's attempt to intervene in the public sphere.

2

The Women's Room and the Fiction of Consciousness

"I wanted to start a revolution."

— Marilyn French.

"[*The Women's Room*] really wasn't a recommendation to go out and join the Women's Movement."

Marilyn French's *The Women's Room*, famously marked on the cover with the promise "this book will change women's lives," was published in 1977 amidst a barrage of mainstream media comment. It spent months on the bestseller lists in 1978 and 1979 and was turned into a made-for-TV movie in 1980. During this same period, women's centers and feminist groups across the U.S. produced hundreds of newsletters and dozens of magazines, newspapers, and journals, almost all of which carried book reviews. Mention of French's text is conspicuous by its absence from these counter-public sphere publications. *Ms*, perhaps the nearest thing to a mainstream-oriented women's liberation publication at the time (certainly the only one that had significant corporate advertising revenue), gave *Room* a brief and dismissive notice ("soap opera and low-budget soap opera at that"); otherwise any references in feminist publications are alienated asides about French's and her publishers' cooptation and exploitation of movement ideas ("heralded in the straight press as 'the women's liberation novel' which only proves how little reading of women's books . . . they do").[1]

Finally, and again in *Ms*, Lindsy Van Gelder wrote an article exploring the gap between feminists' disgust with the novel and its immense popularity with nonfeminist readers; the novel speaks to

47

the trapped housewife, she concludes, because it allows her to explore the consequences of changes she might make in her life without requiring—as the women's movement is imagined as doing—that any such transformation actually occur. As a reader explains: " 'You can sort of live through things in the book that you're not yet prepared to deal with in life.' "[2]

In the account of this reception history given by Marie Lauret in *Liberating Literature* (1994) a subtle reordering has taken place. Rather than an original and contemporaneous response by feminist readers, negative reaction to the novel becomes a belated, and by implication oversophisticated and elitist, failure to recognize the effective text, which has itself become an originator of feminism:

> Because it made many of the ideas of American Second Wave feminism accessible in popular form to a wide audience of uninitiated readers, *The Women's Room*, in spite of its later feminist detractors who dismissed it as a political and literary misconception, was and still remains one of the founding texts of the modern Women's Movement.[3]

Lauret's rescue of French's text—the latest in a series of remedial readings by recent feminist critics—is undertaken on both political and aesthetic grounds.[4] She argues that it is through a reworking of realism that the text is most politically active: in documenting the difficulty of the quest for authentic selfhood, it exposes the inevitability of failure under patriarchal social relations. It thus becomes possible to reconnect the assertions of the publisher's marketing drive, French's own claims to agency, and feminist criticism: *The Women's Room* emerges as the paradigmatic case of a book that changed lives.[5]

This reclamation is interestingly consonant with the reception given the text by the official public sphere on original publication: there too it featured as an inciter's manual, the catalyst and signal of profound social change. In exploring the nuances of this configuration of interpretations and reinterpretations, I want ultimately to raise questions about the version of history that feminist criticism is creating through its account of *Room*'s cultural function, and the purpose that such a refigured history might serve in the current pedagogical and political climate of institutional feminism. Why are the earlier negative feminist responses currently being discounted in favor of a reading of the novel as populist transformer of the mainstream? *The Women's Room* as paradigmatic instrumentalist text is also an ideal vehicle through which to interrogate the processes of mediation between feminist text and world. If both contemporary feminist critics and 1970s cultural gatekeepers grant *Room* transformative properties, what exactly is being changed, and how do they know? My argument here will not be with the notion that women, reading *Room*, may have experienced a shift of consciousness. I take seriously the accounts of transformation that women have told at the time and since.[6] Rather, I want to focus attention on the significance of those transformations for larger, social units: if individual women's lives are changed by French's text, how do those changes impact on the world—the world that, ultimately, feminism aspires to transform?

THE WOMEN'S ROOM AND THE OFFICIAL PUBLIC SPHERE

The Women's Room not only was a bestseller but was always marketed as such.[7] Its cultural effects therefore have to be understood as mediated both by this commodified production and by responses to that production as well as by responses to its self-positioning as feminist insurgent in a hostile official public sphere. The text's publication history and the social significance of its success were matters of contemporary discussion: the novel was not merely reviewed and its author interviewed, in themselves attentions not generally paid to authors of bestsellers perceived as "mass market"; stories about the auction for the paperback rights and the account of how the manuscript found a publisher also made their way into the *New York Times*.[8] The tone of this commentary indicates that the topic is not merely neutrally "hot" but the cause of some anxiety, an anxiety expressed in terms of a perceived incongruity between commerce and high cultural aesthetic standards as a measure of literary excellence. The earliest responses to the text sought to explain and limit its impact by defining it against the presumed purity of literature as simply a bestseller, a commercially generated phenomenon as commodified and constructed as Cabbage Patch dolls; but as the novel continued to sell, proof of its involvement in market mechanisms seemed insufficient to contain its influence. The cultural gatekeepers consistently respond to the novel as if it were a call to arms directed at a vast collective mass:

"It may well . . . rouse the submissive from their lethargy."[9] Such a political intent is linked directly to a failure of literary value; indeed, the main focus of reviewers is on *Room*'s failure to be fiction at all. But the reviewers also seem to be aware that this weakness will not necessarily lead to the novel's failure as instrument of change—aesthetic disqualification does not render it worthless in other registers of value.

Helen Yglesias's review in *Harper's* is an example of the attempt to deploy aesthetic disqualification against a text seen as conceptually and categorically unruly; while Yglesias would appear to be addressing the literary shortcomings of French's method in assimilating *Room* to self-help manuals, there is more at stake in this argument:

> Marilyn French hardly seems to understand what it is that fiction *does*, what it is that's singular about fiction, a subject too complicated for a review but summed up in the simplified notion that whatever hell fiction is putting its characters through, if it's good fiction it is always giving the reader pleasure. If not, why read fiction at all? There are more efficient ways of gaining information. [original italics][10]

We note that Yglesias addresses here not the high culture audience for whom aesthetic pleasure is an established value (to whom presumably she would not have to explain what it is that fiction does, or at least not in the "simplified" terms that are appropriate for a review where things must not get "too complicated"), but some middle rung of persons whose aspirations must be directed toward that source of cultural capital. In defense of the value of pleasure, Yglesias is uneasy enough to hector, emerging from the whimsical dialogic mode of reviewing convention, in which cultured individual speaks to cultured individual, into the rhetorical relation of teacher and pupil, informed and uninformed. What will happen if her audience does not realize that boundaries have been violated, if they merely eat French's message, "much of its storytelling laid out on the table like a prepackaged meal served directly from commercial containers"? For Yglesias sees that French's fiction does *something*, despite its possible failure to provide aesthetic "pleasure": "The very force of her conviction and her energy carries her to a kind of victory. One's objections are almost overcome. Ridiculous to complain."[11] The complaints that Yglesias does in fact go on to make are, again, about literary deficiencies; but this recuperative effort only partially occludes the "victory" that French has achieved, apparently against the will and the better judgment of her reader. Yglesias's support of "pleasure" as the proper function of fiction is of course appropriate to a defense of the properties of the refined aesthetic gaze, just as the demotion of a reading of French's text to the tangible physical consumption of a "prepackaged meal" places the taste satisfied by *The Women's Room* on a lower level on the Kantian scale. But such categorizations fail to solve the problem of the text's obviously *having* a function, one that refuses to stay metaphorically recontained within the pressed plastic compartments of the TV dinner. For if it is indeed food then it is convertible into energy. Refusing the stasis of the distanced aesthetic experience, French's audience consumes not to induce stupor, seemingly, but as a prelude to action, to "a kind of victory."[12] Yglesias's various aesthetic disqualifications do indeed disqualify, but they fail to disempower. Instead of a dichotomy reasserted between high and low culture in which pleasure becomes both its own reward and confirmation of social status, Yglesias's Canute-like pronouncements suggest the emergence of an alternative system of value in which instrumentality is the dominant term.

Christopher Lehmann-Haupt takes up the problem of a power to move readers that can be disassociated from the affective properties traditionally attributed to fiction. In his *New York Times* review, the meaning of "fiction" and its truth value shift as Lehmann-Haupt searches for the category that will best contain the explosiveness of the novel. Initially he assimilates *Room* to reportage, defining it as "a history of women from the 1950s through the '70s," and remarking that "the best compliment I can pay it is that I kept forgetting that it was fiction." This equivocal praise for documentary verisimilitude simultaneously suggests the innate superiority of the unequivocally fictive. Yet Lehmann-Haupt's concluding evaluation uses "fiction" to suggest not the sublime creativity of art but the falsity of illusion: "But finally I was able to convince myself that Miss French's novel is after all a fiction. . . . I suspect that my insistence that *The Women's Room* is finally only make-believe has less to do with critical judgment than it does with a desire for self-protection and comfort. *The Women's Room* is a book women are going to read to relieve [*sic*] the stories of their lives."[13] The shift across the spectrum of definitions available for

fiction allows Lehmann-Haupt to confirm the aesthetic inadequacy
of French's work, but only through the revelation of its instrumental value as "reliever." While *The Women's Room* is safely deaestheti-
cized, by the same token it has become more clearly a politically
active instrument of resistance.

The keepers of culture may be disturbed by the instrumental
power of *The Women's Room*, but such force can yet be defused if it
can be shown to be misdirected. *Newsweek* defines a very specific
audience as the novel's target:

> [T]his . . . novel . . . is meant to stand for the experience and aspirations
> of a whole class of educated women. . . . [T]hese are the women who
> formed women's groups in the 60's. . . . French has put all the revolu-
> tionary fervor and misanthropy of those days into Mira's story. . . . [I]t
> perfectly reflects the ideas of a certain kind of woman at a certain point
> in the history of the decay of marriage as an institution. . . . [Those
> who] . . . have tried motherhood and housewifery, have hated the en-
> slavement they found in those hoary institutions and have gone on, in
> middle age, to look for freedom in work.[14]

By providing a sociological profile of the text's audience, the review repeats the move whereby *Room* has no universal aesthetic
meaning, but instead addresses a transient and material need. This
disaffected (menopausal) crowd of consumers will, furthermore,
be doomed to disappointment by a product they purchase under
false pretenses: "simplistic both as art and politics . . . *The Women's
Room* ought to make a bundle for its publisher. . . . Already a paperback house has plunked down $750,000 for reprint rights, rec-
ognizing that this may be, for liberated women, what *The Other Side
of Midnight* was for their unreconstructed sisters."[15] By assimilating
Room to romance, the reviewer has deprived the novel of even the
limited power of simplistic politics; as romance, its popularity is
interpretable as up-to-date feminine escapism rather than rebellion. By virtue of its commercial success, *The Women's Room* reveals
its complicity with commerce. As popular culture, its instrumental
power turns out to be the power to create desires to be satisfied by
consumption of the text rather than by any more dangerous move
into the world outside.

Reviewers go to considerable lengths to redescribe the formal
structure of *The Women's Room* and its effects on readers as those

pertaining exclusively to the most commodified version of mass culture: fiction as food; fiction as romance; fiction as self-help and therapy. What all of these disqualifications have in common is the picture of cultural production and reception that is implied, in which an all-powerful and manipulative machinery creates a product that is passively consumed by an audience incapable of discrimination or resistance. The claim, "This is not fiction" works in effect to guarantee the nature of the text's relation to its audience as well as the nature of the product itself. As consumer product, it is narcotizing for its audience. As a product itself, it is controlled from elsewhere, an extruded item on consumer capitalism's conveyor belt. The absent literary other, "fiction," against which *The Women's Room* is defined is thus not only "free" in the sense that it is imagined as apart from commercial machinery, it is free in the sense that it is agent rather than acted upon, discourse that uniquely has the power to produce culture. *The Women's Room*, the reviewers suggest, is produced by culture and hence incapable of intervention because it is without agency.

In this respect, the assumption underlying the official public sphere reviewers' account of mass culture is similar to that of the Frankfurt School: it reproduces a passive audience, one whose consumption of mass products reinforces acceptance and integration with the status quo. However, this analysis is, in the hands of the reviewers, itself a strategy of hegemonic reinforcement. It is a strategy that covers over an alternative vision of mass culture in which subaltern publics can use popular culture forms as a means to contestation of hegemony, an alternative vision the reviews at once animate and repudiate. The monster of mass taste, constructed and fed by an insouciant, profit-oriented industry—she who eats the bestseller—is the lesser of two evils; behind her lurks another female gargantuan, the monster of a female mass possessed of collective political intelligence.

The reception of *The Women's Room* in the public sphere, then, while it seeks to assimilate the novel with narcotizing commodities at the same time imagines it as instrumental. The novel's publication coincides with both changing expectations about women's social and cultural role and an organized political campaign against such changes and perceived gains—contemporary feminists, in common with other observers, saw the late '70s as the beginning of a backlash against feminism (ERA was in the process of being defeated; Reagan was in the process of being elected on an anti-feminist ticket). The novel is seen as both the reflection of the movement of a body of women into the public sphere and its means: whatever the actual processes involved in creating the contemporary adjustments in women's public position, this process is imagined by the reviewers as propelled by contestatory cultural interventions such as *The Women's Room*. Their defense of an aesthetic standard and a universal public sphere is based on the perception that French's text can constitute a threat, embodying a change in the nature of how debate is conducted as well as in the makeup of the public sphere. The convention of privatized address, author and reader bonded in interpretative communion, is overwhelmed for institutional readers by an address to a group. Even while actual readers are apparently hearing a voice that addresses them as isolated individuals in the domestic enclosure, reviewers imagine an audience conscious of collective relation—as if this were indeed a text that takes its mainstream audience and relocates it in a new cultural context, an oppositional context from which women, newly aware of themselves as displaced from the centers of power, newly conscious of collectivity, seek immediately to reenter and transform the mainstream under a different grouping.

The images of female rebellion, disorder, and threat that recur in these reviews are a dense, multilayered signifying network, for they refer both metaphorically to mass culture and literally to a mass of actual women, individually and collectively demanding change. The reviewers construct the revolutionary mob they fear; at its head walks French as a monstrous Madame Defarge, a *tricoteuse* who knits an endless, shapeless text into which are woven the misdeeds of the cultural *ancien régime*, a text that incites her mass of female readers to collective frenzied disorder.[16]

THE WOMEN'S ROOM AND FEMINIST THEORY

Evidently, the possibility of the feminist text as an instrument of change is a belief held in common by feminist and nonfeminist readers. The interdependence of the social program of the second wave of the women's movement and its cultural production is a widely acknowledged relation, and generally a celebrated one:

without the proliferation of feminist culture and cultural sites, it is said, there would have been no movement.[17] Fiction, in feminist histories of the movement's development, is no superstructural extra but a primary cause: fiction served both an epistemological function, having the power to depict "things as they are," and as a means to the explication and creation of a feminist subjectivity.[18] Both by redefining old knowledges and by creating new ones, fiction is seen as creating the feminist public from the (previously atomized) woman reader.

This analysis exists in parallel with another almost equally consistent strand of thought: along with a celebration of the power of the pen comes an awareness of the power of the marketplace to control reception, distribution, and interpretation of the pen's production. The novel is envisioned as a potential agent of feminist transformation, but it is also seen as infinitely available to hegemonic manipulation. These two positions emphasize different angles of view of literary production: on the one hand, the novel as agent of change is seen in the first instance as a narrative mechanism. The guiding question to ask of a text is, therefore, a question of form, of what kind of narrative changes lives most effectively.[19] In its purest form, such a theory renders questions of production and reception irrelevant—the encounter between reader and text is absolute. Like a gel-coated pill, the feminist text slips unchallenged through mainstream or counter-public sphere to reach the reader's bloodstream with its message unalloyed. From a different angle of view, one that privileges the site of reading and production, a text is defined by, or at least overwhelmingly implicated in, its context, and the question of overriding concern becomes the placement of writer and publisher in counter-public sphere space. Such a theory authorizes and requires the production of feminist counter-public spheres and their texts; although alternative spheres and products are always in their turn available for cooptation, the potential always also theoretically exists for the emergence of further spheres and other, less contaminated texts. In practice, feminist discourse operates under both assumptions simultaneously: in particular, the aspiration toward and belief in feminism as a universal truth relevant and available to all women implicates counter-public sphere theorists in populist gestures, allowing credence to the idea that a text that begins its journey outside the mainstream (even if only by virtue of the writer's credentials) may be powerful enough—both in terms of narrative mechanism and because of its authentically alternative origins—to survive as transformative agent in the official public sphere.

However, such a text needs a methodology that distinguishes it from other mass market forms—a guarantee, as it were, that it is different enough from the popular text of which feminism is historically suspicious. That *The Women's Room* was successful in presenting itself as such is clear, but the structure of belief involved here is submerged. In investigating this difference, it will be helpful to distinguish French's popular fiction from other mass market forms. While Felski reminds feminist critics that texts can be both popular and oppositional, we know that this is not necessarily their tendency. Searching for signs of resistance in "women's" popular fiction, critics point to a text's capacity to incite and feed unsatisfied desire; hence Tania Modleski's account of the romance as both arousing, as well as diffusing, dissatisfaction with "the order of things," or Constance Penley's account of Star Trek 'zines as expressing women readers' fantasies of alternative sexual and psychological identities.[20] In seeking for ways of identifying romance-reading as cultural critique, Janice Radway largely abandons the text as locus of resistance in favor of the act of reading itself, which both ameliorates absences in readers' personal lives and announces their right and intention to address those lacks. To read romance—in Radway's account, an activity typically requiring long stretches of time, a refusal of other (domestic) tasks, and a corresponding suggestion of pleasurable compulsion—is both to point to and to amend the unlivableness of the housewife's role. Yet reading for Radway—or the fomenting of desire for other cultural critics—is never other than an individual solution, making no claim to address a social structure. The step between an implied cultural critique (which takes the form of withdrawal in order to allow fantasy fulfillment of desires unassuaged by how life currently can be lived) and cultural activism remains even in Radway's most optimistic formulation of popular culture's possibilities one that readers will not take for themselves unless critics intervene to "lead" them into the realm of the social.[21]

Like the suspended animation reported in romance readers by Radway, anecdotal reminiscences of the reading of *The Women's Room* are of an extended epiphanic experience, conveying an impression that the daily routine was arrested for as long as it took to read this (long) novel. But contemporary interviews with readers suggest that reading *The Women's Room* did not lead to a Marcusean reinscription of domestic harmony: "'I'm not an angry person. . . . But as I read, I became furious at things I didn't even know I was angry about. It scared me. And my husband was really irritated. He said, "Every time you read these feminist books you get bitchy." ' "[22] This difference lends weight to Lauret's claim that the feminist realist text produces a sense of disjunction in its reader. The romance produces an alternative world with which the reader experiences pleasurable identification; the appeal of reading lies in the created world's difference from the real of the reader's life. The process of reading *Room* seems to be one of identification also, but this time there is no disjunction between text and world but rather an uncomfortable recognition; the identification produced is unpleasurable, and hence what the reader experiences is anger.

The divergent consequences of opening *Room* and a Harlequin title support the assumption of difference of political valence between the feminist and the nonfeminist text, but this does not address the specifics of how *Room* achieves its effects, or answer Resa Dudovitz's assertion about bestsellers' function: "Women's popular fiction may incite rebellion at home, but it will never cause social upheaval because of its emphasis on the personal."[23] *The Women's Room* presents itself as the text that will give the lie to Dudovitz's opposition between personal and political consequences. It is able to do so because it invokes consciousness-raising, the essential methodology of second-wave feminism, as its structuring principle. Both in terms of its narrative trajectory (the hero has her consciousness raised) and in terms of its announced project in relation to the reader, *The Women's Room* is a fiction of consciousness, and this is crucial to its claim to the status of transformative text.

Consciousness-raising operates to politicize personal experience through an individual's recognition of general patterns that obtain within and between groups and classes of people, and through the recognition of such patterns as socially constructed and socially functional; it creates collective identity between previously isolated individual subjects. Consciousness-raising is central to how reading can be theorized as becoming social change because it both privileges the individual as site of knowledge and action and, at the same time, mediates between the individual and the social, reproducing the individual *as* the social. Faced with a consciousness-raising text, therefore, we are faced with a text that claims to dissolve the divide that Radway's romance reader cannot cross, for the individual whose consciousness is raised cannot rest within the uniqueness of her own experience: it has meaning only as it resonates with the experiences of others.[24]

The plausibility of *Room* as a feminist text does not lie only in its apparent capacity to collectivize the isolated housewife. In addition, the antiauthoritarian bias of consciousness-raising intersects productively with prevailing notions of how reading happens. Consciousness-raising theorizes the individual's path to enlightenment as undertaken freely, without coercion or external pressure. One cannot have one's consciousness raised by fiat; revelation cannot be imposed from above. Although the phrase is sometimes now used to describe a proselytizing activity—when an activist speaks to a group of social workers on disability rights, for instance, she is said to be "raising their consciousness"—such a usage is profoundly antithetical to the original model for the structure of the process; the individual's unprompted agency in her own enlightenment was a necessary condition.

Consciousness-raising is a theorizing process, therefore, but one deeply suspicious of both authority and theory. The assumption that trustworthy knowledge comes only from collective processing of shared experience informs French's self-presentation as a writer. She figures herself not as author(ity) but as a member of a vast virtual consciousness-raising group of suburbanites with whom she will share her life: "I wanted to tell the story of what it is like to be a woman in our country in the middle of the twentieth century. . . . I've been there."[25] The fiction of consciousness escapes from the danger of imposing enlightenment from above by virtue of its authorial positioning within the mass to whom it speaks. Its authority (the right to speak) and its enabling lack of authority are thus based in the same quality—the narrator's equality of experience with her readers. Avowedly writing a polemical text, French must distance herself from all generalization, writing a blueprint that cannot acknowledge itself as such but rather operates under the guise of praxis, as a nontheoretical guide for the housewife's escape: "I wanted to start a revolution, and you can't move average housewives by theory. They want to know realistically what's going to happen when they take a tiny move here or there in their own lives."[26] It follows from this assertion of a neutral, noninterventionist discursive possibility that reading is not construed as involving submission to the ideology of the text, but rather as a free encounter between equals. The conditions for consciousness-raising can be reproduced by and in the reading experience. So although by the mid-seventies activists had concluded that giving talks about women's liberation to groups of the unenlightened was bad politics, merely reinforcing precisely those authoritarian ways of transmitting knowledge that consciousness-raising was designed to challenge, they continued to write novels in which women were depicted as discovering and being converted by feminist gospel. And although feminist theory was alert to material conditions as rendering mythic and unstable the "common ground" of womanhood, it nonetheless continued to invest in consciousness-raising as a context-blind, exportable methodology, one equally available and applicable to all cultural situations.

In her influential 1980 *Feminist Review* essay "Are Women's Novels Feminist Novels?"—which still represents the critique that more recent critics must address—Rosalind Coward locates *The Women's Room* outside the boundaries of feminist fiction on the dual grounds of its "immense commercial success" and its failure of textual innovation: "There are compelling similarities between 'novels that change lives' and contemporary fictional conventions, which should warn us against any simple designation of these novels as feminist."[27] Coward's attack appears to be genre-based, and founded on the assumption that the official public sphere is where hegemony makes the rules and wins. It is also, however, an active political intervention in feminist politics, and as such it asserts specific political priorities. *The Women's Room* is represented as a text that employs consciousness-raising as a faked-up, superstructural addition ("Some of these [popular] novels . . . like Marilyn French's *The Women's Room* . . . even use the practice of 'consciousness-raising' as a framing device"); but even if the mainstream could get it right, it would still be passé: "Consciousness-raising is never sufficient as a politics [and] no longer forms the heart of feminism."[28] Coward's marxist feminist critique is not only of the mainstream but also of feminisms that privilege consciousness-raising as a methodology for social transformation. This is an aspect of her argument that has largely been ignored, for critics who are focusing on the politics of reading are less sensitive to suggestions that are oriented toward what one might be doing *instead of* reading. Coward, writing in a journal, *Feminist Review*, that in 1980 had as many movement as academic links, puts consciousness-raising into opposition against action, as well as relegating it to the past; conversely, for the contemporary feminist critic, much more exclusively locked in to the institution of feminist academia, the capacity that *The Women's Room* offers to read consciousness-raising *as* action serves to legitimate both text and the reading of it as valid politics.

For similar reasons, the difference between *reading* in order to have one's consciousness raised and *going to a group* in order to undergo the same process has also been elided.[29] And while Coward's statements are historically and contextually inflected—her piece was originally addressed to a local movement and intersected with local arguments about priorities for organizing and action—there continue to be important distinctions that should be drawn between reading effects and group process effects.

The roots of consciousness-raising as theory and practice—the weight given to individual experience as source of value and the rejection of external control—can readily be traced back to their emergence from the participatory politics of the American New Left and civil rights movements.[30] The famous slogan "the personal is political," which encapsulates the belief system animating consciousness-raising, represents both an embrace of Emersonian individualism and a significant revision of it: meaning is located in the personal, and the personal interaction with the sensory world, but is arrived at through a politicized understanding of that basic encounter. The rejection of authority is balanced by a belief in collective knowledge that stems from, but revises, individual truth. The individual reader of French's text, on the other hand, starts from and, I would argue, remains in a different position. Fiction is privileged as a nonauthoritarian medium, one in which control remains in the reader's hands. Where a reader acknowledges the power of the text's influence, the process is seen as benign, in contrast to the coercive regime of collective thought: " 'You get sucked in very innocently. . . . You sort of live through things in the book that you're not yet prepared to deal with in life. . . . The point is that it's easier to think about [some of the things that are wrong with the world] through a character than by having some feminist leader give you a speech.' "[31] This reader is not naive about the power of the text, but nonetheless identifies the reading experience as one allowing continued freedom from ideology. Beneath the apparent similarities of a mutual rejection of authority, therefore, lie crucial differences in process and effect. While the structure of the consciousness-raising group imposes a collective viewpoint, reading the fiction of consciousness allows for the refusal of all mass narrative, whether patriarchal or counterpatriarchal. While the group member comprehends her experience in relation to that of others with whom she is in direct contact, the reader can only move between the text and her own life. The consciousness-raising group, finally, produces a theory of how the world works on the basis of communally recognized material conditions, whereas the reader can only act on, or on the basis of, her own experience; the known and imagined self continues to provide the axes between which change is envisaged as occurring: " 'It made me feel as though I'm not crazy, but it really wasn't a recommendation to go out and join the Women's Movement.' "[32] Men wrote to French accusing her of having broken up their marriages.[33] But what kind of social transformation does this imply? Is it French's "revolution," or is it an increase in the divorce rate—a change in cultural conditions, certainly, but not necessarily a wholesale disruption of a patriarchal system of social relations?

READING *THE WOMEN'S ROOM*

Feminist ideas about the novel as instrumental, and the methodology of consciousness-raising, combine to render *Room* plausible as agent of collective transformation, albeit that the feminist counter-public sphere also produces a counternarrative of *Room* as a mainstream appropriative scam. The novel is seen by the official public sphere as a powerful agent of change, and as an instrument of collectivity. It is the more paradoxical, therefore, that the novel itself seems to project no such vision, to be capable of no such imagining, that in fact the impossibility of collective action figures largely in the text. *Room*'s contemporary reading within dominant discourse is in crucial ways a creative misreading through which the public sphere imagines the social transformation it expects, fears, and can control through this projection.

The Women's Room tells of the hero, Mira's, entrapment within womanhood and her gradual and reluctant coming to awareness

of male power and female powerlessness. The story moves, inexorably detailed, through Mira's restricted but innocent girlhood to
the doomed arrival of her sexuality and male incursions upon it.
From these Mira attempts to escape by marrying, thus reinforcing
her bondage by means of social expectation and dependent children. In middle age she is abandoned in the slough of suburbia by
her deeply conventional, but faithless, husband. Mira's enlightenment, foreshadowed by the female networks always operating
amongst suburban housewives, takes place as she returns to school
and finds feminism, women graduate students, and sexual liberation. There can be no happy ending for Mira in a patriarchal
world, however, and she remains disillusioned and alone at the
novel's close.

When *The Women's Room* became a made-for-TV movie, the most
substantial revisions were to the ending. In the original, Mira fin-
ishes the novel washed up, as far out as she can get, walking the
strand at the northern tip of the Eastern seaboard. She works at a
"third rate community college"; her glittering career at Harvard
and her reawakened sense of sexual possibility—the hopes of a
new life—have been reduced to the role of outcast. She is a Cassan-
dra who guards her knowledge of the world alone. In the movie's
ending, however, in place of Mira the disaffected teacher who
stalks the beach making nasty remarks to old men, the film pro-
ducers created a final scene of inspiration from Mira the revered
and successful academic. She looks down from her podium, deliv-
ering her celebrity lecture on women's issues to a sea of eager
young faces. Finally, nearly two hundred years after Mary Wollstonecraft in *A Vindication of the Rights of Woman* imagined an apa-
thetic female audience who slumbered as she exhorted in vain, is
gathered a crowd of disciples, clearly present and clearly listening.
"Women," Mira tells them, "are people who make choices." The
second wave of feminism is at its crest; banners of reform held
high, inspired by a leader's rhetoric, an army of professional
women is about to be unleashed upon the public stage. This rewriting clearly refuses key elements of the novel's insight, where the
"choices" offered by the free market are shown to be unavailable
to Mira. While in the film cultural capital is effortlessly translated
into material economic and institutional power, the original Mira
is denied this ideal insertion into the ideology of liberal meritoc-

racy. The movie literalizes a reformist project, the infiltration of the bourgeois public sphere by the daughters of educated men. Social change is projected onto the screen, its methodology and its results explicit: equality of opportunity will issue in a new egalitarian era.[34]

The film revision is the most visible rewriting of *Room* as effective means to social change: Mira on her podium is a kind of animation of the project of the novel itself, moving a collective audience to collective action. The structure of the text can also be read as inviting such interpretation—the text's refusal of resolution allows the reader to imagine alternatives to Mira's pain and isolation, just as *The Wrongs of Woman* in depicting Maria's defeat at the hands of justice compels into the reader's mind an alternative system. Into the vacuum created by Mira's dissection of the world as a hell peopled with power-crazed men and their female victims, some alternative must come. Yet *Room* does not leave free the utopian possibility of alternative futures and happy endings: Mira's despair is a result of having examined alternatives and found them wanting, of having glimpsed her solution and found it beyond her reach.

In her long journey to enlightenment, Mira passes through a number of stages. Mira's typical story describes, as it must, the socially sanctioned trajectories of her cultural moment's desire: the housewife's path out of the suburbs leads through academia. Mira's story follows precisely the track prescribed by changing expectations over the course of the 1950s and '60s in America. The '50s are, for Mira and reader alike, a dark ages of ignorance from which we have all progressed. Mira's aspirations conform to those of the present of the reading experience: happiness is no longer a home in the suburbs but an education and a fulfilling job. When Mira makes her suicide attempt, after being asked for a divorce, there can only be one solution, cause for a rare moment of affirmation. Mira's friend finds her on the bathroom floor, bandages her wrists, and gives her a drink:

"I kept thinking I ought to care about the boys, but I didn't."

"No, I know. Nothing else matters when you feel that much pain. . . . Listen, Mira, you have to do something."

"I know," she sighed.

"What about going back to school?"

"Yes."[35]

With the ease that only seamless insertion within ideologically nurtured expectations can provide, Mira moves from the intellectually impoverished New Jersey suburbs to Harvard. The reader is rewarded with a teleological progression from cultural poverty to cultural riches at the same time as Mira in her embodiment of meritocratic myth presents no barrier to identification. In *The Women's Room* one goes to school in order to learn, and the best place to go is Harvard. It is at Harvard that one learns to be able to question authority. But to do so one has to inhabit and invest in the structures of that authority.

The narrator's belief is not unequivocal; as she tells it, the return to school is an expectation that experience reveals as unfulfilled: "It was a new life, it was supposed to revitalize you, to send you radiant to new planes of experience where you would get tight with Beatrice Portinari and be led to an earthly paradise" (210). The failure of the earthly paradise is figured as the community college where Mira must teach grammar and fairy tales rather than the glories of Western culture. But if Mira has been rejected by the institutions that perpetuate the cultural hierarchy, she has not rejected them or their standards: the definition of paradise is unquestioned; it is merely a matter of who is allowed to enter. Unlike Mme Defarge, whose response to Harvard would surely be to knit "Veritas" into her woolen text as an ironic reminder to storm and burn the Yard come the Revolution, French has written a text that is as much petition as it is indictment. Thus at her most apparently alienated Mira still reiterates her credentials, those qualities that should have guaranteed her entry into privilege: "I am a good scholar, and in a different market, I could have done decent work" (686). The trajectory of desire follows the path of inclusion within the existing structure, despite the novel's totalized vision of a culture organized around an inflexible binary opposition, male/female, them/us, haves/have nots; opposition is to be resolved by the individual's passage across the boundary rather than by its dissolution or by the definition of any other ground of being.

The text longs for official paradise while it demolishes alternative social possibility. The revolutionary impulse in *The Women's Room* is embodied by Val, the character who operates as a truth-sayer, the extremist against whose views all other characters must test themselves, in comparison with whose radicalism Mira knows herself wanting. She is also an embodiment of expressive freedom, the one who not only speaks out but is also able to sustain a series of torrid affairs. And yet—like Mme Defarge—she encounters a personal tragedy that (fatally) she can accommodate only by seeking revenge not on a personal but on a structural level: when her daughter is raped, Val realizes that all men are potential rapists. She becomes a separatist, disavowing both men and male culture: "I've found a militant feminist organization, and in the future I will work only in that. Fuck the dissertation, the degree, Harvard" (632).[36] Val's move out to what is presented as the lunatic fringe is not a move out of one world into another, from the male to the female, however, nor even a move from male culture to female nature: "There's a bunch of women living in an old house. . . . They get by. I'll join them soon. I don't look for pleasure any more in life. . . . Once I valued it—pleasure, joy, fun—but no matter what I did now, where I went, that is gone for me" (632). The move away from men, from heterosexuality, is a move into absence. Outside culture, outside relations with men, there is no other pleasure, only renunciation. This equation is confirmed by Val's eventual fate: she is shot by police when her women's group attempts to spring a woman from prison; so many bullets, we are told, had been shot into Val's body that it "exploded." It is a graphic reiteration of the inevitability of sacrifice of the self for those stepping outside cultural bounds. Like the beach on which Mira walks, fringes are associated with death.

Mira's own departure from Harvard is the reversed form of Val's repudiation: it takes the form of a visit, as it were, to the interior, a return to her origins over a Christmas break; when the petit bourgeois relations are assembled, she realizes both their narrowness and bigotry and her own difference. Harvard, she realizes, has changed her, lessened her bitterness; she has become "rounder." Cultural capital fills you out, makes you a more complete person; on the other hand, the outside of belonging cannot be imagined except as a place inimical to maintenance of bodily integrity. Val disintegrates when she evacuates from her body all the elements of "male" culture. Mira has internalized that culture (she is rounder because she has swallowed it) and hence she takes it with her wherever she goes. It is the desire that fills her, driving out all other possibility.

In *The Women's Room* the place of utopian longing is taken by the desire not to know, the desire to be able to return to the fold. Mira's cultural escape, from New Jersey to Harvard, proceeds in step with stages in her political development. Gradually she becomes aware. What Mira is left with, what she indeed is at most pains to hang on to in the face of a hostile world, is a capacity for knowledge, specifically a capacity to see through comforting illusions and social fictions to the systematic oppression of women by men. But the narrator, Mira after enlightenment looking back through the course of the novel on the journey toward her of Mira-before, looks back on hopes blasted. There is no possibility of political escape comparable to the journey to Harvard. Knowledge is not power:

> [I]n a way it doesn't matter whether you open doors or close them, you still end up in a box. . . . There's Mira with all her closed doors, and here's me with all my open ones, and we're both miserable. (11)

Mira is left contemplating a world whose relations and structure she understands but which she is powerless to change. Those who attempt change collectively, as Val does, are destroyed by the system and, perhaps more significantly, abandoned emotionally by Mira and the narrator as fanatics incapable of personal relations. The text seems to know that before the social, the individual is powerless. What is the effect on the reader of an encounter with such a vision? How is the reader to step back from the abyss of pessimism into which Mira has fallen? The revision—that retreat from the final brink—that the novel encourages the reader to perform is an individual one bound by the quest structure of the narrative. The text shows women that they should wise up to exploitation, stop looking after everybody, and go to school, but it also issues a warning—avoid the extra step out into the wilderness, because there is no "there" out there. The imaginary journey of the reader is taken through identification with Mira's predicament and ends in her imagining herself/Mira an alternative ending: not alone, perhaps not at the community college. What this structure of exploration does not seem to encourage in the reader is the imaginative construction of an alternative: the world is to be known, not changed. With careful planning and good advice from Mira, the reader may be able to find a niche within the earthly paradise. The impossibility of change is perhaps the novel's most radical perception, for it contradicts what is after all the official public sphere's most fondly protected article of faith, that real change can happen within the boundaries laid down by dominant discourse.

THE WOMEN'S ROOM AS OBJECT OF HISTORICAL KNOWLEDGE

Here is the reading scene for *The Women's Room* in 1977: As a form, the fiction of consciousness sets out to replicate the mechanism of consciousness-raising, and the rhetoric of feminist enlightenment confirms the status of fiction as a radicalizing tool. For readers, the process of individual discovery and self-knowledge occurs not only in communion with the text but also communally, insofar as this experience is being repeated by other women and is announced in the media as happening simultaneously to tens of thousands of others. Meanwhile, the official public sphere is reflecting back the popularity of the novel, and the effects of its reading, as a mass uprising.

It may seem contrary to question so unified a perception of *Room*'s social consequences, and yet there are, as I have tried to suggest, problems with this account. Unanimity of opinion does not, moreover, necessarily guarantee truth; it may only indicate a particularly useful cultural narrative, one that provides a comforting structure of meaning for individual relations with the social. In the above reception of the text, the difference between knowledge and power, between individual and social action, has been erased. The invisibility of this difference is made possible by a culture deeply invested in the ideology of individual freedom, and specifically enabled by a particular combination of cultural circumstances. Dominant and feminist counterhegemonic discourses intersect to produce a common vision: the cultural narratives of consciousness-raising and the instrumental text, and the public sphere's vision of a mass on the move both act to create the expectation of change, the apparent conditions of its possibility and the belief in its currency. Nonetheless, the individual reading journey is distinct, both in structure and in effect, from that undertaken within a consciousness-raising group. *Room* can imagine no possibility of social change, only a personal trajectory of inclusion or expulsion. Without the collectivized theoretical perspective provided by the group, the reader resolves disjunction and injustice in these same terms. It is in the public sphere that a collective meaning is attached to these atomized reading experiences, while individual readers resist that description and identification, declining "to go out and join the women's movement." The relation between "this book will change your life" and "this book will change our lives" is finally one made metaphorically, in the imagination of cultural commentary. Such an imaginary connection will indeed have cultural consequences, but its failure to address institutional structures suggests the fragility of any change thus organized.

One swallow does not make a summer, but neither, outside the power of aphorism, do a mass of swallows. The question *The Women's Room*'s history raises is whether feminist criticism wishes to continue to privilege the mainstream feminist text as weapon if what even the most widely disseminated and apparently successful such text produces is a flock of career-bent swallows, but no cultural summer in which they—or the rest of us—are to live.

I have sought to render visible two positions which have become veiled as feminist criticism narrates itself and its own origins within academia. The first of these is *The Women's Room*'s identity *as* a mainstream text, an identity that had implications for its reception and effects. The second, obviously connected to the first, is the existence of an original counter-public sphere reading of, and resistance to, *The Women's Room* as a transformative agent of social change. Although French proclaimed her intention to shift her public, in effect converting her audience from readers in an official literary public sphere to active participants in another, oppositional forum, counter-public sphere readers saw a different mechanism at work. In the view of these readers, *Room* can only reinscribe its readers within the economy of that sphere. While such a reading is problematic insofar as it fails to acknowledge any oppositional possibility for popular texts, the suspicion of dominant means of containment is a useful reminder that, from the margin, *Room*'s claim to define and explain women's personal and political truths is seen as another act of exclusion. The counter-public sphere response to *Room* is, in effect, another way of hearing the position that is present in the text through Val. The novel does give Val both voice and space; the margin is not literally excluded from the text. But Val is finally discredited, literally and metaphorically exploded. She functions as otherness, against which Mira as representative of universal woman defines herself. The counter-public sphere is not, then, either a livable alternative or an utopian possibility for *Room*, but rather a marginal, emptied-out region which serves to render the center definably itself—and the place to be. The narrator remarks, in her final moments of anomie, "This is not the world I would have wished" (686); but French's women on the move have nowhere to go, for no other place convincingly exists.

In the current topography of feminist discourses, feminist criticism has itself moved into the mainstream: the margin is again in some danger of ceasing to exist, for to acknowledge a position marginal to one's own is to acknowledge oneself as potentially (and of course falsely) hegemonic. I do not accuse feminist criticism of deliberately silencing our opposition, but it is nonetheless worthwhile noticing the interestedness of our operations upon the texts of the feminist past. The usefulness of *The Women's Room* for contemporary feminist criticism lies in its redemption of the mainstream as arena of struggle. Such a vision would have been neither attractive nor necessary to an earlier cohort of feminists, who saw themselves as occupying unequivocally counter-public sphere positions. As feminist criticism recognizes itself as both operating within academic institutions and created by those institutions, it becomes desirable to have models for successful intervention in the official public sphere. Further, *Room* as transformative text, the novel that changed a million lives, sustains the culturally enabling narrative of the usefulness of feminist fiction itself. And given the importance placed on fiction in the women's movement's accounts of its gestation and progress, it is not only feminist literary criticism but also women's studies in general that is strengthened and legitimated by confirmation of fiction's power to transform.

The Women's Room—and feminist criticism's operations upon it—illustrate a continuing process which requires an equally continuous self-reflexivity: the production of interested narratives of feminist history and of feminist fiction as political agents. The consequences of the placement of a feminist text within an institutional context will be reflected in changes in how the text is available to be read, and to what end. In the classroom, French's text will no longer be expected to have the power to transform its readers, who will be distanced from it by this institutional placement; it will instead be read as an example of a *formerly* instrumental text. Such a position renders the status of effective instrument unassailable, because such a status becomes permanently attached to the text as part of its historical meaning. The history of dispute, and of the interests that combined to define *Room* as effective instrument, will tend to be repressed. To keep open the question of the text's agency, and to allow continued visibility to the structures that create its institutional placement, feminist critics need to interrogate not only the valences of narrative structure but also of their own and others' reading positions in culture.

3

Jodie Foster Slays the Dragon: *The Accused* and Rape in the Reel World

The Accused (1988) was uniformly presented—by director (Jonathan Kaplan), stars (Jodie Foster and Kelly McGillis), and screenwriter (Tom Topor)—as an explicitly feminist film which aimed to challenge and radicalize its audience; it was received in these terms by reviewers.[1] It is the possibility of such a project, its means, and whether the film succeeded in these aims that I want to address here. The issue is more complicated than simply the question of whether a commercially successful film, emanating from the center of "dominant cinema" (Annette Kuhn's term for Hollywood and its products, encapsulating an ideological function as well as the genre's control over the means of production), can disrupt social structures in a radical way. For a feminist film, the problem of representation of women without their attendant objectification is central; *The Accused* intensifies this problem by depicting, in detail and at length, a woman's violent gang rape. Woman's visibility as object, and only as object, has been the starting point of feminist critiques of cinema: rape is the apotheosis of the voyeuristic male gaze, at once an acting out of the mechanism of cinema itself and of the oppressive rules of sexual difference. It is clearly necessary to consider, therefore, whether it is possible for an avowedly feminist film to escape from the structures it seeks to critique, and especially whether it can do so by self-conscious reiteration of those structures of both seeing and being. Finally, but perhaps most significantly in terms of the film's interaction with its own historical moment, *The Accused* is a refiguration of an actual rape case. The original case was successfully prosecuted but resulted in disgrace for the victim and a vindication of the rapists within their local community; while the film reheroizes the victim, it also tries to produce a shift of view of a more profound kind so that guilt is lodged as much with the audience as with the rapists themselves. The film thus makes a claim for itself as a mechanism for social change: *The Accused* attempts to rewrite history the way it should have been in order to change how history will be. After the film, in other words, an audience should be produced that would not have participated in the original rape on which the film is based, nor in the victim's anathematization.

Feminist film theory addresses how cinema reproduces culture. Laura Mulvey's originary assertion that cinema reproduces "a world ordered by sexual imbalance" in which "woman . . . signifies male desire" remains in place as a foundational statement of the problem, despite her solution having been repeatedly challenged.[2] If woman is the embodiment of sexual difference, the ground for the creation of male identity, then her cinematic representation in the body seems necessarily to reassert her specularized status. Mulvey suggests that the economy of woman as object for the male gaze can be disrupted by a refusal of the pleasures of narrative, and by a detachment of the audience so that identification with the camera's look (and voyeurism) become impossible; in alternative cinema, audiences can be made to refuse the illusion of the camera lens' innocence. Historically, however, it is criticism and not film that has sought to reveal the mechanisms behind the camera. Rather than providing a different product for the same audience, that is, feminist film theory has attempted to be and to engender a different audience, an audience that is at least self-conscious about what it is seeing. This may be a necessary limitation. Teresa de Lauretis provocatively suggests both that the power of cinema is such that it functions as the twentieth-century equivalent of perspective, defining a way of seeing that renders all others historical, irrevocably defining authenticity, and that "narrative and visual pleasure constitute the frame of reference of cinema."[3] If cinema indeed constructs how we know what we know, tinkering with its mechanisms can offer no escape: if scopophilia *is* cinema's perspective, then feminist activity can only usefully concentrate on how the audience interprets and responds to its inevitable pleasure in looking, rather than on trying to practice or theorize a cinema that is non-cinema.

Criticism has also concentrated on how classic cinema works to promote a lack of self-consciousness on the part of the spectator, and how that willing suspension of responsibility for looking participates in the reproduction of culturally appropriate ways of seeing. Central to this effort has been a focus on the spectator as gendered, both exposing the male beneath the apparently universal, and attempting to theorize an angle of view for the female spectator that might both acknowledge and undermine her participation in her own objectification. It has been suggested that "gender imbalance" can be disrupted through shifting multiplicities of identification, but these theories imagine only shifts across a given boundary defined by sexual difference. The dislocations of gender offered by *Paris Is Burning* (1990), for example, where the subject/object on view may refuse to position her/himself in relation to these boundaries or may claim to occupy a different position than that assumed appropriate by the viewer, and where in consequence no spectator's gender positioning can remain quite stable: this is not the ground on which *The Accused* or its contemporary film theory plays out resistance. The battle is to be fought over a more essentialist ground, woman as subject and as male object(ification).

It is worth noting, in addition, that the film viewer is consistently envisaged as both the passive recipient of dominant ideology and potentially its critic. It has always been theoretically possible for feminist viewers in particular to reject the position offered to them. Tania Modleski, for instance, has suggested that "patriarchal" film can operate as a consciousness-raising tool, generating anger in the viewer by means of the revelation of women's oppression: "The 'truth' of patriarchal consciousness lies in feminist consciousness and depends precisely on the depiction of victimized women."[4] The feminist does not, in other words, have to stop seeing films, as Mulvey's suspicion of the effects of pleasure once suggested. Provided (by feminist film criticism?) with a means of resistance to the mechanisms of her own internalization of objectification, she can remain at a distance from the forms of femininity that reach out their tentacles from the screen.

It is this critical context that allows *The Accused* to be read simultaneously both as an example of dominant cinema, a film that requires a feminist analysis to expose its culturally complicit structure and constructions, and as itself a feminist film, one that seeks to participate, despite its Hollywood provenance, in a project of social criticism.

*　*　*

In March 1983 a woman was gang-raped on a pool table in a bar in the Portuguese section of New Bedford, Massachusetts, while onlookers shouted encouragement. When the story broke, response in the community and in the local and national media was immediate and intense. Local women organized a candlelit march and a Coalition Against Sexist Violence. The bar closed abruptly, never to reopen. Newspapers editorialized about a culture in which indifference to the suffering of others was apparently endemic, while feminist commentators saw the pressing issue not as a disinclination to get involved but rather the reverse, the bystanders' *willingness* to participate. A total of six men were indicted on charges of aggravated rape. They contested the victim's version of events, claiming that she had "encouraged [their] initial advances." The victim issued a statement to the press: "There have been a lot of lies told . . . about me"; "Wait for the trial for the truth to come out."[5]

The trial began a year later, to enormous media coverage. The event was broadcast live on local cable networks and nationally on Cable News Network (CNN), the first trial to receive this treatment. Despite the defense's attack on the victim's credibility and the confusion of stories that emerged in testimony, four of the six men accused were found guilty of aggravated rape; two, also charged with the same offense on grounds of having cheered the rapists on rather than physically committing rape themselves, were acquitted. "The system worked," in the words of the District Attorney; the juries' verdicts (there were two trials running simultaneously, since some of the defendants were expected to incriminate each other), together with other successful prosecutions of gang rape occurring at the same time, were interpreted as indicating a change of attitude on the part of the public, a new willingness to stand behind the concept that consent to rape was not given by a woman's presence in a bar, or her drunkenness, or her previous sexual history. However, the trial and its coverage raised issues that were not resolved by the trial verdict. First, the acquittal of two "onlookers" provides no positive evidence that the encouragement of others to rape is seen by the public as a criminal act: the aspect of the case that initially caused the most comment and seemed most to provoke cultural self-examination thus remained moot. Second, the victim's trust that at the trial the "truth" would "come out" was not rewarded by the result she presumably had in mind, the vindication of her story and her character. Although the verdicts were interpreted as meaning that the trial juries believed her story over those of her attackers, there was another jury listening to the evidence, one that judged against her. As soon as the trial opened, it became clear that "now that the testimony is coming out," the local community had shifted sides: her story was read as a tale of her willingness, her incitement. Early comment, immediately after the rape, places moral impropriety at the scene of the action: "That bar's reputation [is] not good"; during her testimony, however, her neighbors weren't letting their children play with hers because they "think she's bad," shifting the locus of evil onto the victim. The victim's ordeal (at the trial) thus consisted partly in the totality of media exposure of the event and its power as spectacle—everyone in New Bedford, it was reported, watched the trial "instead of their favorite soap opera" —partly in the fact that the exposure included disclosure of her name and made her readily identifiable, but also specifically in the consequences of this exposure—she was revealed but not vindicated: "People will avoid her and look down on her. . . . [s]he'll probably have to move or change her name," a neighbor remarked. After the verdicts, she moved out of the state.[6]

Through its investigative process, the operation of justice produced two forms of guilt, that of the defendants and that of the victim. This effect on the victim—not in itself unusual in rape cases—was exacerbated and complicated by a third issue. The shifts in community feeling seem to suggest an absolute polarization between feminist issues (such as violence against women) and ethnic issues (such as discrimination against ethnic minorities). The Portuguese community felt they had been targeted by a discriminatory judiciary and responded by forming a Committee for Justice, which raised bail money for the defendants and monitored the trial for discriminatory practices. Increasingly, the defendants became identified as "their own" by the local community, in distinction both from the judicial structure and from the victim herself, despite her also having a Portuguese background (as did the District Attorney prosecuting the case). The evolution of this bipolar cultural configuration is encapsulated by the three protest marches prompted by the case: the first, within a week of the rape, was a women's event, coordinated by both Portuguese-American and other women to express a gender-defined outrage. The second march was organized after the first trial to protest the two guilty verdicts given; it was twice the size of the first march and its theme was "Justice Crucified." The third march was a response to the second trial; its focus was again to protest the verdicts, but it was also a celebration of the two acquittals. This was the largest of all, again more than twice the size of the previous protest, a sufficient event that the mills of New Bedford had to close for the afternoon because employees left en masse to attend. The men found innocent were reported as receiving "a heroes' welcome" amid signs that read, for instance, "She is the one who deserves a prison sentence." Although some attempted to negotiate between the two classifications of oppression, in the public mind, as evidenced by their comments and slogans and their cheers or boos in the courtroom, it was a choice between identifying with the victim as a woman and condemning the defendants as violent men, or identifying with the defendants as Portuguese in conflict with a racist judiciary—this latter identification at the same time requiring that the woman be condemned as the criminal party. The visibility of their oppression required her guilt, not just that of a discriminatory legal system that applied its rules unequally. On the other side, condemnation of the men was often expressed as, and operated as an outlet for, racist sentiment. It is the confluence of these two issues that I think accounts for the peculiar virulence of community comment on the woman's action.[7] She is seen as an agent of an oppressive system, a traitor to her people because she has betrayed them into the hands of the enemy. All female action thus has a tendency to become suspect, and female independence incompatible with ethnic integrity; condemnation came impartially from both official and private sources—a priest defending the men declared, "She is to blame; she led them into sin," while a female spectator at the trial also commented, "The fact is a decent woman would not go into any bar to buy cigarettes."[8]

The New Bedford case, and its reconstruction in *The Accused*, is crucially about the cultural consequences of visibility, both for the object seen and for the spectator. The original trial was itself produced, and read by its viewers, as entertainment, as the kind of viewing that is without guilt or consequences for its audience. Given the judicial framework, the media coverage was an exploration that could be justified simply by the search for truth and justice. And the mechanism of the camera in the courtroom, apparently merely recording the action as it happened, created an impression of transparency; the live coverage, claiming verisimilitude by virtue of its constancy and immediacy, obfuscated the creation of meaning involved in its presence. Another layer of exposure also of course took place in the courtroom, the recreation of the scene in which a woman was watched by an audience while being raped. The function of this retelling is theoretically a shift of enquiry onto the members of the bar audience who watched, for it is the alleged rapists and encouragers to rape who were on trial. And yet the focus of attention repeatedly swung back to the question of what they, as audience, *saw,* just as in the community's response to the trial judgment was made upon the victim. The barroom audience was not consistently scrutinized by either trial proceeding or the coverage itself, for the issue for both jury and viewers was that of the victim's behavior and its cultural meaning. They occupied the place of the men in the bar, looked out of their eyes: seeing how that woman was behaving, what would you have thought of her?[9]

The Accused takes up the issue of visibility on several levels. In itself the shift into realist cinema is potentially generative of consciousness, for an avowedly fictive representation is produced in place of the news camera's claim to unmediated reflection. The claim to transparency by which realism itself operates also presents a problem, however, one the film seeks to solve by self-reflexivity, by combining the act of looking with that of looking at itself looking. This process takes the form, in the first instance, of making explicit that the visibility of the victim is an intrusive exposure, both in the rape and in its legal investigation. The film also attempts a refocusing of the gaze onto the audience of the spectacle, bar patrons and cinema patrons alike. Its project is a complex and potentially far-reaching one, for it thus attempts to use a voyeuristic medium to disrupt voyeuristic activity, to repeat that activity in such a way that its participants, the audience, are rendered self-conscious and have to look not at the object of their scopophilic look but at themselves as voyeurs. But in producing a critique of visibility as a mechanism of judgment, the film first concentrates on the damaging effect of *invisibility,* on what the gaze of judgment cannot, or will not, see.

The Hero's Path to Visibility

The narrative strategy of *The Accused*—its way to solve the problem of the New Bedford case's aftermath—is, in the first instance, individual empowerment. The victim recovers the self that rape has taken from her. The plot of the film follows Sarah Tobias, whom we first see fleeing from the bar where she has been raped, and who experiences further trauma through the institutional responses to her attack—in her hospital examination, the insensitivity of the Assistant District Attorney (ADA), and a plea bargain that lets her attackers plead to a lesser charge—but who finds resolution to fight back: shout at the ADA, throw out her insensitive boyfriend, attack a man who taunts her with having seen her being raped, and tell her story triumphantly in court when the cheering crowd, rather than the rapists, are on trial.

The first sound that Sarah makes in *The Accused* is a scream as she runs from the bar, of which we see only the outside, toward the camera. When the scene cuts to the hospital, Sarah can only whisper; her voice is hoarse almost to absence. In the clinical whiteness of the examination room smooth women professionals are politely interrogating her about her sexual history. As her feet come out of the stirrups, the overhead light passes blindingly across her face; we see her shut her eyes in pain. It is clear that Sarah is a person being tortured, a body in pain. As Elaine Scarry has pointed out, pain is invisible unless represented; it remains within the body of she who experiences it, without external referent and hence inaccessible, unconfirmed, to those outside. Speaking of pain inflicted by both disease or injury and torture, Scarry writes what might stand for *The Accused*'s manifesto: "The failure to express pain . . . will always work to allow its appropriation and conflation with debased forms of power; conversely the successful expression of pain will always work to expose and make impossible that appropriation and conflation."[10] The film takes on the task of rendering Sarah's pain visible: the camera renders to the audience what is invisible to the people examining her and what she cannot say for herself. Initially, the spectator sees Sarah in a state of language deprivation: the narrative of *The Accused* consists of her pursuit of her own lost voice, the personal narrative that will "externalize, objectify, and make sharable what is originally an interior and unsharable experience."[11] Thus Sarah must contend with those who would silence her, and with those who have a different interpretation of her narrative, before she can achieve the authority of her testimony in court. Like the New Bedford victim, Sarah can say, "Wait for the truth to come out," and it does, rendering her pain a matter of common knowledge and interpretation, releasing her from it. On the courthouse steps after the verdict, Sarah's return to a normal, quotidian life is evident: "I want to go home and I want to play with my dog." How is *The Accused* able to produce such a resolution, such freedom from pain? Or a personal narrative that acquires the power to control the representation of experience, as the New Bedford victim's could not? How can Sarah's acquisition of the power to define be translated into the real world somehow, when we have seen that the actual audience to the trial resisted any such transfer of discursive power to the victim?

On the *fictive* level, Sarah's story is easy to believe. *The Accused* provides for two ideologically powerful and culturally convincing stories, the individual's search for self and the triumph of universal justice; the two gradually coalesce, lending each other credence by their joining. Sarah must first come to recognize her own silence and consequent misrepresentation, and the mechanisms that produce it ("there have been a lot of lies told about me"). Here control over the media of representation and over a class-bound judicial system is seen to be intimately connected. She looks up from her job as a waitress to the TV in the corner of the room to find that her attackers' lawyers are claiming that she was a willing participant; the camera cuts to a fraternity house where a crowd watching the same broadcast cheers one of the rapists—one of their own. Sarah learns of the plea bargain that substitutes a charge of "reckless endangerment" for rape by the same means; this time the camera cuts between Sarah the waitress, taking a break alone after closing time, and the ADA who has made the deal, Kathryn Murphy, serving her guests an elaborate dinner in her spacious apartment—playing at being a waitress in her leisure time. Class has clearly been a factor in Kathryn's decision that a working-class woman who was drunk and interested in sex at the time would make a bad witness for the prosecution. Sarah embarks on a series of self-assertions, stages toward disproving Murphy's decision that "she isn't good enough to be a witness": first she confronts Kathryn over her dinner with having silenced her and with having ig-

nored the issue of her overexposure: "You don't understand how
I feel. . . . I'm standing there with my crotch hanging out for the
world to see." Then she goes home and cuts her hair before throwing out her insensitive, boorish boyfriend.

It is an impressive series of actions: in successive scenes Sarah
expresses her anger, alters the meaning of her appearance, and
rids herself of a bad relationship. She may not be happy (yet), but
we have to admire her strength, and one might think she has done
enough, overcome enough narrative obstacles, sufficiently arrived
at a place of awakening to herself. But this has been preparation,
it turns out, for the questing hero's battle with the dragon. The
self has to be reempowered through the institutions that have silenced her. When we next see Sarah she is being propositioned by
a man in a store (the dragon personified: he has a scorpion tat-
tooed on his arm) who insists he's seen her somewhere before.
Sarah denies it, but he has recognized her as the woman he saw
being raped in the bar: as Sarah tries to start her car he taunts her,
gesturing obscenely, "Do I know you!" Continuing her mission
of self-assertion, Sarah drives her low-slung sports car at the soft
underbelly of the dragon's truck and ends up in the hospital. As
the long scene of exposition that follows makes explicit, self-assertion is insufficient, for it cannot guarantee control over discourse.
The ramming of the truck is an empty gesture because it has no
impact on how Sarah is seen. As Sarah, made aware of her powerlessness after literally hitting her head against the institutional wall,
tells Kathryn Murphy: "He figures I'm a piece of shit—why not—
you told 'em that. I never got to tell nobody nothing. You did my
talking for me." Sarah has been raped but it is by the system that
she has been screwed. In the absence of juridical protection, another, misogynist, discourse can reign unchecked, as the ADA
learns when the dragon tells her what he sees:

Dragon: "She's a whore. Last time I saw her she was doing a sex show."

KM: "You watched?"

Drgn: "Bet your ass I watched—she put on a great show."

KM: "I thought she was raped!"

Drgn: "Raped? She fucked a bar full of guys then she turns around
and blames them for it? Listen, lady, she loved it. She had an audience;
she gave the show of her life."

Sarah's silence—the original lack of language of the victim confirmed and legitimized by the legal system—has converted her ordeal into spectacle; the silenced body becomes the site for "appropriation" by "debased forms of power." The reiterated "show" establishes that control over the scene and its interpretation remains with the audience before whom the passive body is displayed. Sarah can be as assertive as she likes: the dragon of community perception goes on seeing what it sees. (What is also suggested here is that the existence of the audience *in itself* converts a rape into a spectacle; this is an issue to which I shall return below.)

The dragon's version of events reveals that the system within which Kathryn operates has failed to control representation; the failure allows Kathryn's gender allegiance to triumph over her commitment to her professional position. This conversion is necessary if Sarah is to succeed, for Murphy has access to the institutions of authority, to the site of meaning production that is the law court.

It is because Kathryn realizes she must prosecute the onlookers (of whom the dragon is one) in the interests of institutional protection of the rights of the individual that Sarah "get[s] to tell [her] story." Control, the authority to define interpretation, is equated with the right to speak: telling automatically confers authority. The central drama of the courtroom is the recounting of that story, first by Sarah and then as a voiceover by a witness who was in the bar, Kenneth Joyce, who testifies on her behalf. By describing the experience, Sarah is able to make manifest that what she experienced was rape, not a "sex show"; her pain becomes objectified, externalized, and sharable by jury and audience. The cross-examination takes up the issue of the visibility of her pain, seeking to establish that her lack of consent and her suffering did not exist because it was possible that no one saw them: "Did you signal to anyone? Did anyone see you struggle?" But the ground has already been won—Sarah's personal narrative has established truth; it remains only to confirm her authority by the jury's verdict.

The film enacts a crucial exchange between visibility as spectacle and as self-expression. In gaining or regaining a voice, and thus the power to tell a story, is exposure negated? Does the body in pain become less a spectacle because it speaks? In the terms offered by *The Accused*, this is apparently so: the closure the ending offers, as Sarah returns to her private, domestic enclosure, is apparently also the closure of the voyeuristic eye. A story told and a verdict delivered, the obscenely visible is erased, and in its place is the visible self, boundaries re-created through her apparent control over representation. The issue, thus, is not representation but self-representation, not visibility but self-revelation. And yet this resolution—reassuring as it might seem—is undercut by the film's own urge toward producing visibility as exposure rather than as the individual's structuring of what she wants us to see.

The account I have so far given of *The Accused* might seem to provide only limited justification for my earlier assertion that the film is a feminist revision of the New Bedford trial, for on the one hand a story that is redeemed through the judicial system and that redeems that system by granting it the power to reestablish an individual's sense of self would seem both politically and narratively reformist, at least, and possibly conservative, its gesture in the direction of feminism confined to the issue of consent and the insertion of a female hero into the classic narrative model, its solutions eschewing the social for the individual.[12] Furthermore, to produce a guilty verdict as resolution to a rape victim's problems would seem to ignore the most pressing issues raised by the original trial, particularly the failure of the New Bedford juries' verdicts to address or redress the community's rejection of the victim and of those verdicts themselves, and the negative effect of the victim's telling her story on her credibility.

The hero's successful self-assertion repeats the New Bedford victim's naivete about who is in control of such narratives. The empowering of the individual requires that she be able, in the end, to produce (her own) truth. The film denies its own awareness that truths are produced by the institution—in this case the court—rather than transcendently by the individual. Sarah's pursuit of "telling her story" recognizes that a story told in court has power conferred by the court, but the film represses the extent to which the story that is produced in the courtroom is the court's story rather than Sarah's unmediated representation of her experience. In fact the loss of control that is consequent on telling one's story within a given structure is revealed by a scene in the film in which Murphy discovers from Sarah's friend that, before the event, Sarah joked about sleeping with one of the rapists, a "fact" that Sarah has not disclosed. Murphy is enraged by this concealment; "What other surprises have you got waiting for me?" she demands, automatically assuming her right to know everything. The film re-

presses this transfer of power from teller to institutional interpreter by excusing it as personal—Sarah apologizes to Kathryn
and the incident becomes an illustration of their difficult cross-class
relationship rather than a comment on how the authorship of a
story will pass out of its original owner's control as soon as it is
told.[13]

THE HEROINE'S PATH TO INVISIBILITY/EXCESS VISIBILITY

The Accused can be read, and even presents itself, as Sarah's epic,
but this reading requires that the reenactment of the rape scene
be passed over. Narratively, at least in terms of the "search for
self" story, there is no need for the rape scene to be depicted:
Sarah Tobias is vindicated and her right to define the truth of her
experience reasserted through her courtroom testimony. Her authority is produced by the fact, precisely, that her words are unac-
companied by any visual reenactment that confirms the account
she gives; her words stand alone and are sufficient. But the film
goes on, to provide a visual reenactment of the rape and to provide
the narrative of a witness: Sarah's word is not, the narrative progression implies, sufficient after all; in order to be convinced, we
must not only hear about the rape from another point of view, we
must also see it for ourselves.[14]

The film's capitulation to the necessity for visual reenactments is
not without resistance: Kaja Silverman's statement about female
lack of authority in film appears to be directly contradicted by Sarah's testimony: "The female subject . . . talks a great deal. . . . But
her linguistic status is analogous to that of a recorded tape. . . .
[t]he participation of the female subject in the production of discourse is nonexistent."[15] Sarah not only tells her own story, she
tells it for the first time (the audience has had no previous blow-
by-blow account), producing a narrative that has both original authority and the persuasiveness of the telling of first-person experience in a confessional, individual-centered culture. If in the
courtroom Sarah is embodied (defined by Silverman as a state of
confinement—and obviously, necessarily, a state of confinement in
a particular gender) she is barely so, although her face and voice,
reacting minimally to the events she recounts, might be said to be
a synecdoche for the body and its assault, both of which are off-

screen.[16] But Sarah's authoritative voice is immediately superseded by another, Kenneth Joyce's testimony given as voiceover. Here Silverman's account seems to gel with *The Accused*'s production of meaning: "The capacity of the male subject to be cinematically represented in this disembodied form aligns him with transcendence, authoritative knowledge, potency and the law."[17] It is Ken's testimony upon which the verdict turns. The defense summation attempts to establish that Ken is an anomaly, one who needs to "purge himself" of "his own sense of guilt"; this attempt to feminize Ken by suggesting homosexuality, self-hatred, and masochism—to reembody him by departure from the universal status of manhood—is countered by the prosecution's claim that he is, on the contrary, the average man: if he is that, of course, then his disembodied voice will carry a telling and sufficient weight in law. Not only does the authority of the voiceover succeed to and leach away control of discourse from Sarah's testimony; Ken's disembodied narrative also presides over Sarah's reembodiment, her reconstitution as body without words. In fact, although the film is apparently constructed around Sarah's path to reclamation of her self, that process is ultimately secondary to another and potentially much more radical aspect of the narrative design. Sarah's individual authority is sacrificed to a greater good: the enabling deconstruction of the authority of her audiences.

Kenneth Joyce's testimony and the depiction of the rape scene itself are in service not to the heroine's needs but to the film's attempt to challenge the audience into self-consciousness. Within this frame, the viewer's identification with Sarah as protagonist is a necessary prelude to a challenge to that identification. The film defers the depiction of the rape scene in order that Sarah be established as a sympathetic character, one with whom the spectator will be likely to side whatever his ideas about rape and provocation to rape; we need to believe in Sarah so that when she is raped we see the event *as* rape: as inexcusable, criminal, antisocial violence. And yet equally we must identify with Sarah so that when the rape happens, and in the buildup to it, we can move away, or feel ourselves intermittently move away, from that identification into a loss of sympathy, into another angle of view, that of the onlookers.

As soon as Ken's testimony begins, the flashback also begins. Although the flashback is narrated through Ken's voiceover, the camera is not limited to his point of view, or to an exposition of events that he could have seen. The camera angle is low as Sarah comes into the bar, as Ken tells us she looks "sexy," as she sits in a booth with her girlfriend. Then it moves away and watches from across the room as Sarah plays pinball and flirts with two men whom we recognize as two of her rapists. Then, still from across the room, the camera watches Sarah as she dances alone, the straps of her tank top falling off her shoulders. The challenge to the audience at this point, before the rape happens on screen but with foreknowledge of the event, is to refrain from thinking that, stoned and dancing "to steam your specs," in the metaphor for arousal of the *Time* reviewer, Sarah is asking for what she's going to get.[18] The odds are in fact stacked against the audience here, for even if convinced that sexual "provocation" cannot condone sexualized violence, it is impossible not to wish that Sarah were not doing what she's doing, given what will happen next. The rape itself is depicted as sufficiently brutal, violent, and dehumanizing that it becomes clear that no one could be understood or misinterpreted as to be asking for *that*; the disconnection between sexual provocation—possibly asking for something—and violent rape is explicit. It is also a relief to the audience—Sarah can't be blamed for a response to her behavior that is so obviously inappropriate.

However, this moral test is not the main focus of the scene. For, as Sarah dances, the camera begins to watch those who are watching her. As Danny, the first of the about-to-be rapists, moves in to embrace her, the camera swerves to pick up the dragon (he of the scorpion tattoo) moving out from behind a pillar. The point of view switches and we watch from his angle as Danny tries to kiss Sarah and as she begins to protest. The camera circles, focusing on the crowd that is beginning to gather and then cutting to their view as Danny hoists Sarah up and onto the pinball machine. As the rape proceeds, the camera alternates between looking at the onlookers and depicting their voyeuristic look, interspersed, once Sarah is finally trapped, held down and making only inarticulate sounds, with lurching handheld shots from her angle of vision. As the violence escalates and the cheering and incitement get louder, this structure remains in place: the disengaged camera, observing the cheering, gesturing men; the rape from their point of view— our point of view—featuring the churning buttocks of a succession of rapists; and the blur of faces seen from underneath as from Sarah's position on the pinball machine. The multiplication of

angles enforces a series of positions on the audience: if the shots of
the cheering crowd as it were from outside and the shots from
Sarah's position both in their different ways enable and require
the spectator to keep his distance from the mob, the view from the
onlookers' standpoint replicates, and invites participation in, their
participation. The combination creates self-consciousness, an
awareness of complicity with the onlookers even as, given the
safety of occupying other points of view, one condemns the voyeuristic position. Tom Topor, the screenwriter of *The Accused*,
stated that the intention behind the shooting of this scene was to
put the audience in that position of discomfort, so that the viewer
has to ask himself, "What would you have done?" and reject the
complicity that the film reveals in the knowledge that he is not
exempt from it, that rejection requires a change in himself as well
as in others, for he participates in a culture where membership in
the cheering crowd is easy.

Contemporary reception of *The Accused* concentrated on these
aspects of the film, on the film in other words as the vehicle for a
message on the one hand about rape as a crime of violence to
which the immorality of a victim does not imply consent, and on
the other about how the spectacle of a rape and an audience's participation in that spectacle is licensed and encouraged by a culture
that confuses sex and violence and that condones and encourages
other forms of male bonding through violent spectator sports. The
film uses sports both as a parallel with the rape scene in particular
and as a metaphor for the structures of the ambient culture in
general—thus, while the rape goes on in the back room, patrons
at the front bar watch a boxing match; as Sarah's girlfriend runs
from the bar they are raising their fists in celebration of a killer
punch. Kathryn's accommodation to and participation in masculine values is likewise established by the siting of her conference
with her boss at a hockey game. Their conversation about the suit-
ability of Sarah as a witness is punctuated by the DA's encouragement of crunching tackles on the ice; they speak of rape and watch
violent sport. This context operates further to disenfranchise the
"cheering squad" in the bar, but also to render their action more
generalized, more likely therefore to be something of which the
film's audience could also be guilty.

Comment on *The Accused* is almost unanimous in agreeing that
the rape's brutality renders it not an erotic spectacle, and that the

cinematic depiction itself is justified by the strength of the message that the film contrives to convey. Reviewers ubiquitously remark on how vivid and graphic a demonstration *The Accused* provides of the feminist truism that rape is "about" violence, not sex. The original intention behind this rhetorical position was to disconnect rape from a sexual continuum, specifically that of consensual heterosexual intercourse; in a culture where women are always presumed to want or need or be persuadable into sex, lack of consent can only be understood if what is in question is not sex at all; violence is a form of attention of which it is conceded most women would not be willing recipients. The rape in *The Accused* is assuredly violent. And even if the brutality depicted were not rape but, say, three men taking turns beating a woman with their fists, there would equally be a gendered element to the scene of male violence and female victimization. Yet rape is, unlike a beating, a peculiarly sexualized form of violence, and one that is seen as performed, again unlike bludgeoning, almost by definition across gender difference and that reinforces that difference (if a man is raped by another, he becomes feminized by the act itself—it unmans him).

To say that *The Accused* depicts simply an act of violence is to lose sight of the rape as by definition an act of violence across gender. Similarly, to claim that the brutality of the act depicted in and of itself guarantees that the depiction cannot be an erotic spectacle markedly misrepresents the cultural meaning of violence and its web of connections with arousal. The depiction of a violent rape may denaturalize violence without de-eroticizing it. This is an obvious truth about which those commenting on the film and its rape scene have been weirdly silent. I saw *The Accused* for the first time in a crowded cinema in which a sizable and vocal section of the audience cheered the rapists on enthusiastically. They were clearly enjoying (whether as sex or violence hardly seems to matter) the spectacle offered on the screen, and probably also the effect their noisy duplication of the film's cheering squad was having on the rest of the movie theater audience. But I doubt that the rest of that audience was simply quivering in silent horror. I was silent and horrified by all the audiences, but the rape nonetheless remained (and this was inextricably part of what constituted the horror) an erotic spectacle. I decline to believe myself the only critic ever aroused, albeit reluctantly, by the film's rape scene. Surely the film's strategy is to place one in the onlooker's position—and that position is one of arousal. The critical silence on this issue can be explained in part as a political necessity—since the film so clearly tells us that the rape is an act of unacceptable violence, to mention its erotic charge would be almost crass, as if we hadn't got the point. But universal repression seems to me to suggest another, more troubling motive: if we as spectators to the film replicate in our own bodies the responses of the cheering onlookers, can we be sure that such repetition is accompanied by some crucial saving difference?[19]

The film has also, particularly in this regard, to be considered as both message and vehicle; attention needs to be paid not only to what the film is understood to be saying but also to how it is saying it. The film seeks to make its own voyeurism invisible (the mechanism); but central to its narrative impulse is the display of the raped body to be looked at (the vehicle). To account for the plot's single departure from narrative sequence—the placing of the rape scene, which chronologically initiates the events of story, last—as necessary to the successful manipulation of the audience's identification with Sarah is to account for it on only one level of structure, for only part of that structure's significance. The film builds up to the rape scene as to a climax and as to a climactic moment: that the two (rape and narrative climax) are conflated suggests that, in narrative terms, the two have to be conflated; the narrative requires and produces the rape as its justification. It's an eroticized structure: what a letdown, if the rape came first; but how much more of a letdown if the rape didn't "happen" visually at all. That the representation is motivated by a message does not remove its impact as representation, or remove the message of the vehicle itself. Nor, of course, does it exorcise the possible (climactic) effects of that representation on the bodies of its audience. By focusing on the film as a re-creation of a possible scenario, one close enough to historical events to acquire an additional gloss of verisimilitude beyond that provided by traditional realist cinematic techniques, the film itself reaches toward transparency. It becomes not product but screen. By concentrating on the question, What would you have done? the audience is able to evade the question, What are you doing now? (And is it the same thing as the onlookers are doing in the present of the film's reenactment?).

Does the film replicate the structures of representation and meaning that its political agenda designs to correct? Cindy Fuchs claims, on the contrary, that the film succeeds in making a crucial distinction: "The film's strength lies exactly in the ways that it shows that women are constantly objectified, but are not objects." This is achieved by setting up "a dichotomy of looking" that "[only] *apparently* gives the viewer authority over the person viewed" (original italics). Fuchs uses the example of the examination room, where the clinical professionals' gaze is revealed as inadequate to encompass or articulate Sarah's situation through the mechanism of the camera's occupation of the other side of the look: "It forces us to see what Sarah (the alleged object of our gaze) sees."[20] Fuchs's account provides a telling explanation of the discomfort and disjuncture the viewer experiences during the hospital scene: the women in the white coats seem to go through all the right moves, gentle and sympathetic despite and around their professional script, and yet, watching, one feels vaguely that something is not quite right. Because the camera sees not only Sarah from their point of view—her bruised body, her face reacting to questions about her sexual history—but also from hers, their arrayed whiteness across the room, their view is undermined. As audience, we become aware of the insufficiency of the authoritative gaze, of the gap (what Sarah is and feels) in their visual account. But the gap is not filled in: our awareness remains a visual one; the inadequacy of the professional view is never articulated on any other level, leaving looks and the gap between them to produce interpretation through disjuncture. It does not necessarily follow that Sarah's capacity to disrupt the process of objectification, in front of a female audience, in the controlled atmosphere of the examination room, before the narrative has gathered pace, can be replicated in the bar before a cheering crowd, when she is the object of a different order of invasive violence, as the narrative drives toward discovery from a particular angle of view. Both content and structure combine to control the disruption of which relocation and diversification of the gaze is capable. In the examination room, that is, we "see" a gap; that is not to say that the audiences to the rape (onlookers and film viewers alike) see the same way.

THE AUDIENCE'S PATH TO VISIBILITY

To sum up so far, *The Accused* appears to consist of an heroic narrative that finds resolution through the operation of the judicial system and a rape scene that undercuts the authority of that narrative by replacing Sarah's voice with Ken's disembodied one played over the scene of Sarah's reembodiment as object. The remaining possibility for disruption of this meta-narrative of escape and reabsorption is provided by *The Accused*'s counterimpulse to reveal the mechanisms of the audience's look. Among those ideological moves most clearly implicated by feminist critics in the reproduction of a patriarchal culture is cinema's claim to be and to allow what de Lauretis in *Technologies of Gender* calls a "safe fantasy," the authorization of what Kuhn calls "lawless seeing": everything is played out and the audience need have no fear, for they can claim both inaction and lack of agency at the same time as they experience the pleasure of a fantasy realized.[21] The disruption of these comforting effects is most pronounced and most explicit in *The Accused* in the filming of the rape scene itself; it is in that scene, of course, in which the issue of the audience is crucial. Here the film makes the look of both audience and camera explicit, and it refuses to allow the audience to disclaim responsibility for the act of looking; it makes clear that neither the fantasy of the cinema audience nor that of any scopophilic crowd is safe.

Is Fuchs's point, that we also see from the point of view of the alleged object of our gaze, sufficient to counter the narrative's complicity with the male gaze's sadistic reduction of the objectified female body? Fuchs contends, in a comment that speaks directly to Mulvey's strictures, that "because we see not only the body but the act of watching that accuses us," we as viewers have to take responsibility both for viewing and for our own complicity. The scene thus "offer[s] no voyeuristic 'visual pleasure.' " Fuchs clearly implies (and in this she follows Mulvey) that there is no saving voyeuristic pleasure; the route to exculpation for *The Accused* is therefore absence of scopophilia if not precisely absence of pleasure. But does our awareness of complicity actually arrest, as Fuchs seems to assume, voyeurism or visual pleasure? It is not hard to imagine being simultaneously capable of "visual pleasure" and aware of and uncomfortable about what that pleasure signifies: the awareness does not cut off the feeling. Guilt and pleasure are hardly mutually incompatible states. Whereas Fuchs's analysis is that difference of view is sufficient to disrupt the structures of visual objectification, it seems to me that *The Accused* reveals that both structure (how we look) and content (what we look at) are integral to the production of pleasure and meaning. And while Fuchs claims that *The Accused* has successfully evaded, despite being a mainstream film with all the accoutrements of realist cinema, Mulvey's famous bete noire of pleasure, in fact she has established only that it is possible to occupy structures of objectification at the same time as being distanced from them. It is possible to shift Fuchs' argument slightly, that is, and propose the audience as a third party with a different view to the construction of filmic meaning. Rather than simply repeating the same dynamic of identification with self and other, subject and object, the self-conscious audience is triangulated with the camera and its object. It may be that the rendering of such feeling self-conscious in itself makes a material difference, that both audience and the overlooked body are placed in a different relation to discourse, that power returns to the body, and is used by the audience, in a different way. Such avowedly polemic cinematic techniques as are used in *The Accused* are all addressed to the cinema audience in the moment of its complicity with the onlookers, and these aspects are all contained in that question, What would you have done?

The Accused attempts a radical dislocation of cultural habit: our comfort as film viewer and our gaze as cultural participant can be disrupted in the same moment by the manipulations of the rape scene. Our discomfort does not depend on absence of scopophilia but only on its being rendered conscious as a mechanism. Thus what is established is a consciousness-raising process. The viewer recognizes the structure that is at work at the same time as continuing to operate within that structure. S/he has internalized the mechanism of looking, and the capacity to stand aside and look at him/herself looking does not arrest or eject that embedded way of seeing. But as with any consciousness-raising process, it reveals as a culturally productive act something that is experienced as individual. At the moment when the structure is most in place, then, *The Accused* contrives a third eye, a way of inhabiting the outside of the objectifying look at the same time as remaining, self-consciously complicit, within that gaze.

Consciousness-raising as a process produces theory: the individual sees himself and his responses to events as part of a social structure. He is thus brought simultaneously to reflect on that structure and to realize that he is caught within it. The consequences of this dual realization are, in feminist theory, also doubled; the individual makes changes in his behavior at the same time as seeing the necessity for change on the level of social institutions and structures. The question then becomes one of identifying the mechanisms by which such changes might be achieved. We have seen that in *The Accused* resolution is provided by the restoration of Sarah's personal integrity, an integrity that is returned to her because the audience recognizes their own guilt along with that of the original audience to the rape. The difference between the New Bedford audience—in the courtroom and the bar alike—and that in the cinema is that the latter is made self-conscious about its looking. Again, the question must then be, is this a crucial, socially productive difference?

In New Bedford, the victim's first account of her ordeal caused widespread sympathy in the community and outside; this response indicates that, prior to the judicial process, she is granted credibility: her personal narrative, despite her rape, carries weight. This first narrative, her account of her experience prior to the trial, approximates most closely to that expression of pain that Scarry describes as necessary to the process of arresting torture and the torturer's capacity to use the body of the victim as a means to his own power. But the victim's move into the judicial process changes the dynamic. The process of investigation in depth, while it results in the guilty verdicts, also at the same time destroys the innocence of the victim. For investigation is also revelation. As the dragon's vision suggests, any "show"—the fact of having been seen—in itself implies consent. The victim is guilty because to be exposed is to be guilty—the judicial invasion that she has allowed by participating in the trial replicates the original assault that she permitted, this time in front of a larger, more demanding audience. Her personal testimony, originally having the power to move, has been disenfranchised by the investigative drive, which insists that the nature of its knowledge has priority and authority over her account.

The judicial process works by evacuation, by bringing "facts" to the surface, by rendering known the secret. The inquisitorial methods necessary to this process maintain a relationship, though no such physical aids to truth or speech may be used, to the use of torture. As Michel Foucault points out in *Discipline and Punish,* in a system where discipline is externally applied and externally visible, there is no such category as an innocent victim of torture. The fact of suspicion sufficient to require an investigation in itself marks a crucial and irrevocable loss of innocence. The New Bedford victim is, by virtue of her need to enter the public sphere of judicial enquiry, deemed to have lost her innocence. All knowledge gained about her becomes, as does confession wrested from the reluctant victim on the rack, evidence with which to convict her: nothing she can say will be exculpatory. She falls under suspicion: by virtue of her presence within the judicial system she becomes a suitable object for examination—for the torture by public spectacle that the media foments and enables.

The social problem that the judicial process fails to deal with or acknowledge is the inexorable conjunction between knowledge and exposure. Both judiciary and jury, the crowd in the courtroom and the community outside gathered around the CNN broadcasts, arrive at their judgment by means of the victim's dissection and revelation. While *The Accused* attempts to change how its audience sees, it does so through the mechanisms that allow the audience to see the same thing. While we may be endowed with a new awareness of the process of judgment, there is no change possible in the reenactment of that process itself. The act of watching the film is thus a reprise of two events: the scene in the bar and the scene in the courtroom. The verdict in the New Bedford case theoretically exonerated the victim from blame; but it did not remedy her exposure. The film gives us nothing different to look at. Thus while it transfers the guilt of looking from the perpetrators to the audience, it leaves the exposure of the victim untouched. If we go on doing the same thing, does it matter how we feel while doing it?

Susanne Kappeler's analysis of the link between torture and art is helpful in clarifying the continuity of the process of trial and film: "With an audience, torture becomes an art, the torturer an author, the onlookers an audience of connoisseurs."[22] This structure can be applied equally to the original courtroom and the film's re-creation of the rape. The distinction between the New Bedford audience and that of *The Accused* is thus not one between real life and art, or art that reorders life, but between unself-conscious torturers and torturers who have been made aware of what they are doing. This is, of course, a difference, but one that requires and countenances repetition.

There are layers of iteration here: *The Accused* succeeds in framing male violence as a cultural form that is both ubiquitous and ubiquitously sanctioned. The film is a reprise of the process of investigation, for it can imagine and construct no other way of seeing. It is an epistemology that requires revelation, the revelation that both the New Bedford trial and the film can only produce as the torture of exposure. Caught within the mechanisms of cinema, obliged always to provide an object as spectacle, *The Accused* can create, finally, only another audience to rape, an audience whose means to knowledge of self and the world require the catalyst of spectatorship at a scene of torture. The only way to understand the operation of voyeurism may be to replicate it, but such replication remains an empty gesture if all it produces is enlightenment without change; the film identifies a mechanism without producing a means to difference.

4

The Visible Margin: Audre Lorde as I/Icon

THE MYTHIC I: *ZAMI*

In analyzing mainstream texts, the feminist critic in search of oppositional possibility can afford to find the reinscription of hegemony, for there is always somewhere else to go, an alternative place to stand. That such a place, the counter-public sphere, does function as a means to contestation, that texts produced from a culturally marginal position are potentially subversive of centrally defined norms: these are reasonable and theoretically supported assumptions. The recent history of American political movements provides compelling evidence of the efficacy of action based on a collective identity conceived and occupied as marginal. And yet the romance of the margin has its dangers: the critical desire to locate an oppositional locale produces both overinvestment and distortion. The margin as site of action becomes increasingly available for commodification as it transmutes into a site of signification, an imaginary location in discourse, which may be only distantly referenced to the social.

Audre Lorde's work serves to illustrate both the power and the limitations of marginal discourse as locus of resistance. I consider first Lorde's "biomythography" *Zami: A New Spelling of My Name* (1982) and then the film made about Lorde's life, *A Litany for Survival: The Life and Work of Audre Lorde* (1995), reading the latter as commentary upon and revision of the earlier work. Enacting and standing for the apotheosis of marginality-as-resistance, *Zami* is the text that, despite Lorde's reputation as a poet, defines her iconic status in feminist criticism. Although Lorde continually reinvents a margin to inhabit, from which to critique, seeking to preserve and utilize the place of authentic exclusion as the place of soothsaying and purity, the reception and reading of this text operate to contain and transform this process, undercutting the marginality that is purportedly being celebrated. *Zami* simultaneously functions, and fails to function, as oppositional, its strategic subtleties recaptured and acculturated. *A Litany for Survival*, filmed over the last years of Lorde's life, both renews the oppositional impulse and recognizes the impossibility of the project of the earlier work. Playing upon, and against, the canonical status that Lorde acquired in the years between the publication of *Zami* and her death, the film revises both self-expression and visibility as goals and strategies of resistance, self-consciously subverting and yet perpetuating the iconic power of Lorde as figure(head) of opposition.

Writing the Afterword to *Conjuring: Black Women, Fiction, and Literary Tradition* (1985), Hortense Spillers celebrates the emergence of a new black women's literary presence, "the palpable and continuing urgency of black women writing themselves into history," one made possible "because there is a strategic audience of heightened consciousness prepared to read and interpret the work."[1] Such work not only redefines the canon, Spillers suggests, but also renders that term itself open to question. In setting up black women's work as both a disruptive and a reconstitutive force, Spillers singles out Lorde's *Zami: A New Spelling of My Name*, just published as she writes, as a particular agent of disruption because of the site of its production: "In the case of Lorde's book, there is more than [a] subtle hint that the publishing center of gravity is shaking loose from its customary moorings as the marginal women's press begins to redescribe the lines of disseminative power."[2] Placing her account of this seismic shift at the end of an anthology that works to locate African-American women's texts in a place of cultural authority, separating out this statement of marginal effect, while at the same time giving *Zami* the power of the last word, Spillers at once points to the insufficiency of academia and broadens its reach. In the event, the original publisher folded shortly after *Zami* was published and the text was reissued by another small, but marginally less marginal, publisher, a reminder of the literal shakiness of nonhegemonic structures of production and dissemination.[3] The subsequent history of the text's reception and its current status provides an interesting gloss to Spillers's expectation of *Zami*'s power to disrupt. Spillers implies three different locations of opposition: the authorship of these new texts; the audience now available to them; and the noncommercial presses engaged in the production and distribution of this different work to a different audience. One could ask for no better example than *Zami*: Lorde's self-positioning as a Black lesbian renders her authorial subjectivity authentically marginal in terms of contemporary discourse, while the early publishing history of *Zami* clearly indicates a marginal audience, both in terms of the original publishers and as suggested by the publication of extracts from the manuscript in journals with a defined counter-public sphere readership.[4]

But *Zami* has not remained outside: current women's studies syllabi and bibliographies suggest that *Zami* has in fact acquired the status of a standard text, where what is to be studied is black lesbian experience; recent conference panels and the MLA bibliography confirm in addition that—while white feminist concerns continue to dominate discussions, and white-authored texts are always in the majority—if black marginal subjectivity is acknowledged, *Zami* will regularly function as its representative, often to the exclusion of other writers and texts.[5] In other words, *Zami* has been absorbed by the white feminist critical hegemony: while the appropriation of Lorde does not disqualify the subversive effects of her work, it repositions Lorde in relation to her margin of origin, as well as reinventing her critique as a transgression that can be accommodated. Spillers's own construction of *Zami* as a destabilizing force is itself predicated upon the dialectical conjunction of a once marginal body of work with the academic institution, the site of creation of cultural authority. Anticipating this development, Spillers herself moves *Zami* away from marginality even as she endorses the necessity of otherwhere as place of production, celebrating a reconfigured world in which the marginal has become central.[6]

Clearly, no marginal position of origin guarantees the survival of a text as an undermining force; no boundary is so far out that it cannot be colonized; no subject position is so marginal that it cannot be recovered. But such shifting cannot simply be read as deauthentification, as if *Zami*, because it locates its validity in its marginality, will be drained of disruptive potential as soon as anyone in a position of cultural authority reads it. The process of engagement between marginal text and authoritative reader is negotiative. One can anticipate certain tendencies within this dynamic: the reader seeks at once to assign the text, reading it into submission (making it, in Barthes' terms, readerly), while at the

same time seeking to preserve the marginal quality that is its particular value. If this reading work is successful, resistance will become a reified, mystic quantity that accrues to the cultural capital
of the critic. The text here can be imagined as resisting the alien-
ation of its oppositionality lest it become an empty sign, signifying
opposition but always rendered safe by the critical gesture of reading and inclusion.

The position of *Zami* in relation to feminist criticism repeats that
of *The Women's Room* in relation to the official public sphere readers, in as much as a radical cultural intervention is recuperated by
cultural authority, but there is an important distinction between
the liberal gatekeepers' and feminists' desire: the latter, even as
they appropriate, wish to preserve and inhabit the marginal properties of the text. A flexible but irreducible essence of margin, both
always available and always open to reinterpretation, thus becomes
available to the critic.

Zami functions in feminist criticism as a signifier of marginality:
by exploring the uses of such marginality for different readers, I
aim to uncover not just critical interestedness but also the ways in
which the text itself attempts to undermine appropriative gestures.
Each generic reading of the text tends to produce *Zami* as not itself
a reading of either the world or the genre, but as the truth of
experience, and thus valuable but historically bound. I try to re-
trieve the specifics of what the text does: does to the history it re-
members and rewrites, to the audience it creates, and to that
audience's sense of the cultural moment that it addresses. While
this is to repeat the process both of appropriation and of seduction
by the romance of the margin, it is a necessary attempt to shift
emphasis from the text as that which is to be read toward a focus
on the text's own readings of the forms and histories it confronts.
This return of agency to the text allows it to be seen not as a static
oppositional nugget of truth, but as a series of resistant (re)read-
ings of cultural formations. The text tries to claim for itself an in-
alienable marginality by virtue of its methodology; it is itself
invested in the romance of the margin, which operates as source
of rhetorical power, despite what I will argue are its limitations as
a strategy.

Zami *and Genre*

Lorde's definition of *Zami*, given in an interview, was "a biomythography, which is really fiction. It has the elements of biography

and history of myth. In other words, it's fiction built from many sources. This is one way of expanding our vision. . . . You might call *Zami* a novel. I don't like to call it that."[7] The instability of Lorde's neologism, its tendency to split apart and recombine differently along its seams, increases the fluidity of the coinage as category. However, despite Lorde's own comment, which points to the creation of cultural rather than personal truth, and emphasizes the fictive nature of her project, *Zami* has been read largely as either autobiography or—a category that overlaps the first but that has generic expectations of its own—coming-out story. Insofar as Lorde's text goes beyond the marginal subject's personal story, to delineate the life of "gay girls" in 1950s New York, *Zami* is also read as history, personal testimony from the margins of the past. To emphasize autobiography over biography, history over history of myth, and coming-out story over fiction is to produce *Zami* as a text of experience rather than of imagination. This gives the text an unequivocal right to speak, as the hitherto silenced subject has the right to be heard. On the other hand, the speaker of the truths of experience is always a naive speaker, one whose words are open to, and need, the interpretative interventions of the theoretically sophisticated.[8]

Lorde does indeed give the reader the personal narrative of a protagonist, Audre, the details of whose family history and personal attributes seem very close to the author's own: Audre's trajectory from Hunter High School to gay bars, library school, and poetry all seem to match more or less with Lorde's own life as it is publicly available through other sources.[9] *Zami* is also densely situated in a web of references to historical events—the Rosenberg executions, Supreme Court rulings on desegregation—and to precise geographical locations in New York City—Harlem stores now changed hands, bars now closed—which both lend it verisimilitude and suggest that Lorde is intending to conjure a specific historical and cultural moment. But while *Zami* is on the one hand about growing up in Harlem, it is also about looking for a home that is not that in which one is born, and about creating a new place of what Lorde calls "sojourn," liminally situated between the irreducible material reality of Harlem and the mythic place of ancestral origin, Carriacou, a West Indian island whose actual place is barely recorded on the colonizers' maps, which cover and hide it, but whose power as site of mythic beginnings is therefore all the stronger. While *Zami* is about the "lived experience" of gay bars in the city in the 1950s, it is also about the lesbian community as theoretical home, about its discovery, and the discovery thereby that home is too safe and too dangerous at once, a place and a concept to be abandoned. It is both practice and theory. The text can indeed be read as history, but it is the history of another time told from a distance, and through the filter of a subsequent history. Lorde gives us the bars in vertiginous detail, but she also gives us a comparative picture of this community, known as one knows it looking back from the early '80s, a moment of disillusion with the ideal of community that the 1950s could intermittently practice but not theorize, and looking back too through the '70s, a time of utopian theory and experimentation about lesbian enclaves as sites of perfect community.

To read *Zami* simply as history, personal or cultural, in other words, is to occlude Lorde's fictive manipulations of the history she is telling (and purports to be telling) and to reserve such manipulations for the interpreter of the text. Reading the readers of Lorde, a consistent tendency emerges: the will to reduce *Zami* to the specifics of a particular genre, a particular time, and a particular personal truth.

Autobiography: Zami *and the Uses of Truth*

Transparency is often associated in the discourse of marginal subjects with an oppositional position; truth-telling is assumed to be synonymous with giving the lie to what a Foucauldian analysis of this oppositional move would define as dominant regimes of truth. What is produced is thus an alternative knowledge that has the power of the unmediated, personal story. Barbara Smith's reading of *Zami* in "The Truth That Never Hurts: Black Lesbians in Fiction in the 1980s" is avowedly motivated by a search for such alternative knowledge: she is in search of positive images, works that achieve both verisimilitude ("how true to life and realistic a work of literature is") and authenticity, by which Smith intends something close to the idea of racial uplift, "a relationship to self that is genuine, integrated, and whole."[10] Although Smith's essay is subtitled "Black Lesbians in Fiction," and she reads *Zami* as not fiction, she includes Lorde's text "because it is the one extended prose work of which I am aware that approaches Black Lesbian experience with *both* verisimilitude and authenticity. *Zami* is an essentially autobiographical work, but the poet's eye, ear, and tongue give the work stylistic richness often associated with well-crafted fiction."[11] It is Smith who reads "biomythography" as "autobiography," reducing the distance between author and protagonist to the merely incidental. Yet while Smith gives terms for her criteria that emphasize narrative realism, the explanation and use of these terms reveal that both fact and fiction are necessary to fulfill them. Although the term "authenticity" has the aura of lived experience, Smith's definition clearly refers to a constructed idea of the authentic, a fictive distance that the term itself seeks to obscure. Just as Smith's equivocation about whether *Zami* is or is not really fiction serves to create an idea of it as a transparent record of personal experience, so her emphasis on the text as autobiographical serves to deny the constructed nature of the identity— the authentic identity—that she wishes to see celebrated in literature. Smith represses the fictive possibilities of *Zami* in order to construct a model of black lesbian subjectivity as a thing of the present, already living and breathing in the text that serves as its record.

The uses of such a reading are clear, but equally clearly the text asserts itself as operating on other levels as well, both generically and conceptually. A reading that emphasizes the ficticity of both truth and self would seem therefore to allow more of the text to come into play. While Barbara Smith uses autobiography, albeit with reservations, as an authenticating measure of facticity, Sidonie Smith locates the improved critical status of the genre precisely in the decay of its assumed claim to transparency, in the resultant capacity rather to see the autobiographical self and its narration as fragile and multiple fictions.[12] For Sidonie Smith, Lorde's differences, her inhabitation of multiple identities—Black, lesbian, mother, poet—that are insufficient singly, is illustrative of the "multiple locales" in which different truths must be seen as simultaneously located. Smith's account of Lorde is sensitive to the complications of a multiple identity; if more than one truth can hold, different identities can likewise be held as it were in suspension rather than be seen as inevitably moving into collision; both experience and construction, both external and internal agency, can be acknowledged as contributing to this subjectivity.

Sidonie Smith's argument can accommodate irresolvably contra-

dictory elements in Lorde's text which in Barbara Smith's framework have simply to be ignored. For instance, Lorde stops the
narrative short before—were this actually autobiography—Audre/
Lorde would become a mother: *Zami* ends in a transcendent evoca-
tion of Black lesbian sexuality and community that makes no gesture toward such heterosexual or heterosocial possibility. Barbara
Smith, reading *Zami* as authentic personal record, simply cannot
acknowledge what in autobiographical terms is a significant absence and possibly even a distortion of an authenticity conceived
as requiring "integration" and "wholeness." But Lorde's dwelling
on a particular location can become in the light of Sidonie Smith's
framing a strategy for locating different truths in different moments and communities of meaning. It is relevant to this difference
of what can be read that Sidonie Smith notes without regret the
apparent demise of the autobiographical contract: "At the current
autobiographical moment, "truthtelling" and "lying" lie close to
one another, affectionately and contentiously intermingling with
and intervening with one another."[13] This rather lesbian-inflected
image (in a text dealing with women's autobiography), and Smith's
reference to *Zami,* allow one to infer that she reads *Zami* as an
autobiographical text in which truth and lying lie in fecund pro-
pinquity. For Smith, lying is a strategy for truthtelling.

In Barbara Smith's account, the "truth" that Lorde produces is
the true uplifting story of Black lesbian survival and its richness.
Audre's search is surely for that wholeness that Smith would have
texts reflect. But Audre finds the completeness of community only
at the moment when verisimilitude is abandoned: the description
of Audre's culminatory relation with Afrekete begins in the minutiae of Black women's parties and bars, but shifts into a different
register as Kitty the Black woman with the almost natural hair becomes Afrekete the goddess: history becomes history of myth:

> I would turn the corner into 113th Street towards the park, my steps
> quickening and my fingertips tingling to play in her earth.
>   *And I remember Afrekete, who came out of a dream to me always being hard
> and real as the fire hairs along the under-edge of my navel. She brought me live
> things from the bush.*[14]

This is a fluidity of form with which Barbara Smith's notion of
authenticity seems insufficient to deal. The mythic nature of

Lorde's account of Kitty and Audre's intermingling resonates with Sidonie Smith's account of autobiographical lying and truth-telling as copulatory: her formulation allows a reading that in fact paradoxically brings Lorde's myth closer to Barbara Smith's truth, for lies thus become lies in service of contestatory truth. But this siting of the text in autobiographical territory alone cannot tell us what regime of truth is being contested, what locale the text itself is (re)-reading. What of lies that seem to be true—that depending on the locale of the reader are or are not accessible as tactics in the contest with a discourse-producing regime? While Sidonie Smith thus releases *Zami* from a fixed position, the text is still not in a position of authority over more than Lorde's protagonist's personal history.

Zami *and the African-American Mother's Garden*

Zami has been assimilated into the matrilineal African-American tradition, codified and popularized by Alice Walker, in which influence is passed from generation to generation with urgency—rather than the anxiety of the equivalent white model. In this account, the metaphorical mothers and daughters of the literary succession, of which the pairing of Walker and Zora Neale Hurston is the founding example and continuing paradigm, overlays another intergenerational mechanism, the transmission of creative energy from each *biological* generation to another. Literally, African-American women are conceived of in this tradition as passing on their mothers' words, bringing forth into speech what those before left unsaid: "We must fearlessly pull out of ourselves and look at and identify with our lives the living creativity some of our great-grandmothers were not allowed to know."[15]

So Barbara Christian is locating Lorde within a validating framework when she describes *Zami* as "a book about Lorde's reconciliation with her mother."[16] What is at issue here is a critical attempt to reconcile Lorde with tradition *as* mother, a tradition of which she has been a wayward and problematic child. Such a project, however, given the naturalized structure of that tradition, produces a reading of *Zami* as more story of origin than myth of origin. The modality of such a reading is, significantly, assimilationist: "reconciliation" is a means of producing truth that seeks to accommodate the text to a given and authoritative model, here both the family of origin and the tradition of African-American women's literature, itself a model of conflict-free reconciliation. A reading through this critical tradition must therefore de-emphasize contestatory truth in favor of what is already in place; it produces the truths of Audre's inward trajectory, but only by allowing the movement of reconciliation to cover other less acceptable resistances.

Lorde, however, defined herself, by virtue of her lesbianism, as outside the literary succession:

> I think a lot about Angelina Weld Grimké, a Black Lesbian poet of the Harlem Renaissance who is never identified as such . . .
>   I often think of Angelina Weld Grimké dying alone in an apartment in New York City in 1958 while I was a young Black Lesbian struggling in isolation at Hunter College, and I think of what it could have meant in terms of sisterhood and survival for each one of us to have known of the other's existence.[17]

Lorde's material experience is of the absence of foremothers, an absence that is both concrete and conceptual—not only are they not present, they are not present to the imagination. *Zami* seeks self-consciously to revise the matrilineal model, substituting mythic African models of self-sufficiency for the heterosexual Black woman's foremothers: "There were no mothers, no sisters, no heroes. We had to do it alone, like our sister Amazons, the riders on the loneliest outpost of the kingdom of Dahomey" (176). What is in the original a heavily naturalized tradition becomes in *Zami* visibly a construction, and a reconstruction in the *absence* of the familial. This refigured line of precursors is a fragile textual presence, present only by virtue of Lorde's power to create it, unlike the textual mothers of Walker's literary heritage who produced material evidence of their existence.

Zami also works on the biological tradition: rather than abandon kinship as a means to community, Lorde refigures her protagonist's relation to her family so that lesbianism too can become an African-American heritage: "[In Carriacou] it is said that the desire to lie with other women is a drive from the mother's blood" (256). Audre's biological mother in *Zami*, what one might call the "mother in the text" as opposed to the "mother of the text," is redescribed as a "Black dyke," but this is a redefinition that has no maternal sanction: "I believe that there have always been Black dykes around—in the sense of powerful and women-oriented women—who would rather have died than use that name for themselves. And that includes my momma" (15). The trope of the matrilineal tradition is effortless transmission of an unchanging cultural word, but Audre's relation to her mother's truth is overtly dialectical and discomforted:

> When the strongest words for what I have to offer come out of me sounding like words I remember from my mother's mouth, then I either have to reassess the meaning of everything I have to say now, or re-examine the worth of her old words. (31)

Where the paradigmatic traditional gesture is the attempt to revocalize one's mother, learning to speak in her voice, Lorde's desire, finding herself speaking her mother's words, seems to be to spit them out. Instead she listens to other voices: Audre's Afrekete-informed vision allows her finally to recognize and interpret words from *outside* the family, the "sweeping woman's tuneless song," which can be read to reveal what the community and its mothers would hide, the family as site of the transmission of violence:

> Momma kilt me
> Poppa et me
> Po' lil' brudder
> suck ma bones. (251)

Audre also repudiates her mother's way of seeing, refusing her strategies for survival and substituting her own: "When I moved out of my mother's house . . . I began to fashion some different relationship to this country of our sojourn. I began to seek some more fruitful return than simple bitterness from this place of my mother's exile" (104). Audre's rewriting replaces the dichotomized binary of home and exile, Grenada and Harlem, with the enabling, but never homely, sojourn, and in doing so suggests that it is the maternal line that is barren, that a new tradition depends on departure from the old ways. The textual repudiation of the mother's words thus applies equally to the "mother in the text," who disappears from the consciousness of the narrative as soon as Audre leaves home; the biological reality has no function in the reworking of the maternal that takes place as Audre negotiates the lesbian community and her place in it.

By foregrounding reconciliation, Christian is able to suggest that

Lorde's desire is to return to the family of African-American women's literature, a model of textual production that reduces to adolescent ranting any discomforting insights that Audre may give forth on her journey: her rejection of her mother, like her abandonment of the Black community in favor of "gay girls" (most of whom are white), can be read as transient rebellion. Audre in this reading finally becomes a good girl, saying what her mothers have said before her. It is she, not the tradition, who becomes the object of revision.

Zami *and the Lesbian Personal Narrative*

The project of the coming-out story is to create a visible, articulate self. As such it is susceptible to the charge of naivete and insufficiency now leveled at identity politics. As a cultural historian of lesbian personal narrative, Bonnie Zimmerman founds both the impulse behind these narratives and the form they take in a particular relation to language: "Contemporary lesbian feminists postulate lesbian oppression as a mutilation of consciousness curable by language. . . . [W]hat [we] identify as the particular, unique oppression of lesbians—rightly or wrongly—is speechlessness, invisibility and inauthenticity. Lesbian resistance lies in correct naming; thus our power flows from language, vision, and culture."[18] Zimmerman is describing a form from a position of both distance and identification; her article is a jeremiad. From the standpoint of 1984, the power of language to create an identity is also its power to generate discourses of power and exclusion: "We must abandon or modify a politics based so strongly on personal identity. Although lesbian feminism evolved during the 1970s as a politics of transliteration, this power of the word has been used primarily to name, and thereby control, individual and group identity."[19] It is as a valuable entry in a now discarded discourse that *Zami* features in lesbian feminist accounts; as excellent example of a form no longer necessary or theoretically desirable, it is thus read into the past.[20]

The centrality of Zimmerman's categories of speech and reading to the foundation of identity could hardly be more explicit in Lorde's account. As a small child Audre is literally speechless until she is four years old for lack of the power of self-authorization: "To this day I don't know if I didn't talk earlier because I didn't know how, or if I didn't talk because I had nothing to say that I would be allowed to say without punishment" (21–22). She finds her capacity for speech through the written word, the need to read producing both a culturally authorized desire and the ability to communicate it in what is said to be her first spoken sentence: " 'I want to read.' "

Audre's invisibility, too, attains the level of textual theme, articulated around the shifts of her various identities, the refusal of the Black community to see her as a lesbian, and the refusal of the "gay girls" of the 1950s lesbian community to see her Blackness. Visibility always carries with it a corresponding dark side, a part that the act of naming obscures in the moment of shedding another light. While Audre's search for self crucially involves the validation that recognition through naming provides, therefore, Audre's dual sense of names as obliterative motivates a journey through language that self-consciously complicates Zimmerman's "individual and group identity." The layering of the 1970s drive toward visibility with later revisions is rendered geographically in *Zami* as two places that enable different ways of being. On the one hand, there is the dualism of two cultures' exclusionary conceptions of identity: "Downtown in the gay bars I was a closet student and an invisible Black. Uptown at Hunter I was a closet dyke and a general intruder" (179). On the other hand lies the grant of presence within a system that allows inclusion without exclusion, presence without definition. In Mexico Audre is visible by means of a sameness that displaces no other: "Wherever I went, there were brown faces of every hue meeting mine, and seeing my own color reflected upon the streets in such great numbers was an affirmation for me that was brand-new and very exciting. I had never felt visible before, nor even known I lacked it" (156). The journey in the text to different places and methods of identity formation parallels the development of feminist theory from a model of exclusive community to one of intersecting sets. Lorde contrives both to celebrate and promote identity formation and to rewrite it as a form of inclusion that has no outside. While the text repeats the gestures that Zimmerman would repudiate, Lorde's use of speech and visibility is also revisionary, repeating in order to critique.

That the text functions as a history of the 1970s, although it is the 1950s that are apparently being described, can also be seen in Lorde's descriptions of the lesbian community. Lorde's portrayal

is both affirming and distancing. It celebrates the capacity to articulate a way of being, represented by the complex and precise codes
of behavior and expression of each fleeting bar. As an act of creation, of visibility, and as the construction of a language, Lorde's
lovingly detailed lists of the minutiae of clothing and hairstyle glo-
rify the capacity to survive and the means of that survival. But the
retrospective return is from a present that is self-consciously other.
The narration comments upon Audre and her friends' lives in that
time in a frame that indicates that the anxieties present are those
of the 1980s, from whence a new articulation of community is necessary:

> The important message seemed to be that you had to have a place.
> Whether or not it did justice to whatever you felt you were about. . . .
>   It was a while before we came to realize that our place was the very
> house of difference rather than the security of any one particular dif-
> ference. . . . It was years before . . . we could appreciate each other on
> terms not necessarily our own. (225–26)

Lorde's insistence on difference marks *Zami* as a text responding
to the same impetus as Zimmerman's jeremiad. The obsession with
belonging that is the subject of Lorde's critique here is a feature of
the search for a unitary identity that Zimmerman identifies as a
common and disabling quality in 1970s lesbian feminism. From
the distance of the 1980s it is the 1970s search for a home that
brings with it an excess of desire for sameness. Thus the "sacred
bond" of gayness is also rewritten here as a position of false secur-
ity, the entrapping bonds of an overpoliced community.
    And yet Zimmerman's doubts about the political consequences
of the tropes of lesbian personal narrative are neither simply
echoed nor simply fulfilled by Lorde's reworkings. If visibility is
finally rendered as nonbinary, it is still, somehow, visibility, retaining the resonance of that term. Neither is Audre about to abandon
the power of speech wrung from a disciplinary, silencing environment. While the narrator repudiates the excesses of the search for
identity, Audre's observing eye details every nuance of the sign
system of demarcation. *Zami* exhibits a disturbing capacity to have
things both ways, to indulge and to repudiate the indulgence. But
in this fashion Lorde avoids the determinate nature of a jeremiad.
In contrast to Zimmerman's 1980s asceticism about the language

of claiming an identity, *Zami* is flamboyant in its occupation of the traditional tropes that cause Zimmerman anxiety.

Reading in the Bar

Thus far I have been staging a debate between *Zami* and feminist critics, in which the latter seek to solidify the text into a fixed marginality, the former always resisting the rigidity of genre. This layer of operations, however, is always synchronous with another, the manipulations *Zami* seeks to perform on the histories it tells; focusing on this level brings to the fore the text's own reading practices. Lorde's re-creation of the gay bar scene should be understood as as much a construction as is the familial tradition in which she is able to redescribe her mother as a "Black dyke" or to locate lesbianism as both innate, African, and "a drive from the mother's blood." In constructing this cultural fiction, Lorde first denaturalizes the African-American tradition by making clear her absence as a lesbian from it, and then rewrites the genealogy so that it includes her. It is an act of active self-inscription that one cannot—and is not intended to—miss. But in the construction of a *lesbian* genealogy, Lorde's redefinitions have been read as more authoritative and (it has become the same thing) more simply a rendition of personal experience. But Audre's account of the bars of her youth is interested and motivated. The bar in Lorde's account is the site of connection and community, despite its being riven by class division and racism: it is the place where a common identity as lesbian is formed and maintained.[21] Class struggle in the lesbian community emerges in *Zami* only in Audre's precise awareness of such differences inflected in infinite varieties of clothing, and in the freedom of some to visit bars only when they chose, rather than when they sought any form of community. It is the possibility of community that runs through all Lorde's descriptions: if there is a fundamental identity anywhere to be found, it is in a recognition of lesbianism in common. In this sense, Lorde rewrites the loyalties of the 1950s as those of the 1970s, when such a communality was overtly proselytized in lesbian feminist discourse. The 1950s thus become a precursor of a later time, at the same time as they also function as a canvas on which to lay out the anxieties of the 1980s.[22]

An important aspect of the 1950s bar scene, one that absorbs

Lorde and other commentators, a constant subject of memory, re-interpretation, and explanation, is the question of role playing. Lorde equates such roles with oppression, and in particular with the oppressive norms of a paranoid and conservative culture; in this aspect, Lorde's account of the lesbian bar world of the 1950s describes multiple fracture, a series of distinctions that merely reflect the hierarchies and oppressions of the world outside:

> The society within the confines of the Bagatelle reflected the ripples and eddies of the larger society that had spawned it, and which allowed the Bagatelle to survive as long as it did. . . .
>
> The Rosenbergs had been executed, the transistor radio had been invented, and frontal lobotomy was the standard solution for persistent deviation. . . .
>
> The breakdown into the mommies and the daddies was an important part of lesbian relationships in the Bagatelle. . . . [T]hose lesbians who had carved some niche in the pretend world of dominance/subordination . . . were in the majority. (220–21)

The absolute consonance of the bar's values with those of the culture as a whole contradicts the claim elsewhere that lesbians were different, the sole seekers after community. This doubleness of description reflects the fact that the bars and their "gay girls" do dual work in the text, representing different times at once. Here in the Bagatelle, where roles and the bars in which they are played out are synchronous with all that is undesirable of the 1950s, Audre and her circle *simultaneously* have available to them an ideology that is clearly that of the 1970s:

> [R]ole-playing reflected all the deprecating attitudes toward women which we loathed in straight society. It was a rejection of these roles that had drawn us to "the life" in the first place. Instinctively, without particular theory or political position or dialectic, we recognized oppression as oppression, no matter where it came from. (221)

It is because of this asynchronous belief system that Audre is called "Ky-Ky," glossed in *Zami* as a term used for those who refused roles. In other accounts of the time, such as Madeline Davis and Elizabeth Lapovsky Kennedy's oral histories of the Buffalo bars of the 1950s, *Boots of Leather, Slippers of Gold*, the same term is defined as meaning the tendency of one so identified to switch *between* roles; it describes an intensification of role play rather than its absence.[23] And this is in effect what Audre is doing: as protagonist in a narrative with at least three different historical angles of view, she does, indeed, play different roles at different times.

Clearly it would be possible to resolve the disconnections of Lorde's various accounts by, for instance, fitting her account together with other versions of the history of the bars, just as one might compare other accounts of social organization in Carriacou against the matrifocal paradise adumbrated in *Zami*. Alternatively, it is possible to recognize both as places of both truth and myth. The fictive rereading that Lorde performs on historical and familial data produces a text that asserts its value as truth at the same time as manifesting its mythic and constructed status. Her biomythography of the gay bar is as much, that is, a myth of origin as the account of Carriacou, rescued in *Zami* from the margins of colonized cartography to be refigured as the original women's community. If Carriacou is a mythic idealization of the rural African women's community, the gay bar in Lorde's account is a mythic idealization of the urban, white one.

The contradictory descriptions of bars and Audre's place in them, working not as static truth but as fictive reconstruction, attack a series of targets. Audre operates within the bar as "Ky-Ky," a position that refuses the "mommies and daddies" structure of the Bagatelle. Outside in the other worlds of New York, however, she comes out as a "bulldagger," the identity that most moves against the sanctity of heterosexual expectation. If neither place is safe or comfortable for her, neither place is safe from her and her discomforting, either. These two roles are irreconcilable, and they are creations of a passing moment: Audre also appears in other dress in other places. They are the external expression not of self or belief but of a different and always differently constituted constant, opposition.

The effect of this perhaps has been to render *Zami* illegible. Insofar as reading involves the pinning of the text into its generic place, then the unreadableness is an intentional effect. Lorde's text exists in a multiplicity of relations to genres and to institutional structures of criticism. It thus replicates the situation of Audre, whereby no one place is ever enough, where only the "house of difference," which cannot presumably be a place at all, will do. But this only produces the text as a three-dimensional *trompe l'oeil*, to stand in

which must be to see many things at once and in which what you
see depends on where you stand. Audre's house, however, is a
house not of multiplicity, or rather not of multiplicity only, but
of difference. The distinctions that the text obsessively re-creates
between and among classes, roles, colors, are not dissolved by proliferation. Nor do the boundaries vary between categories—they
are absolute, for as long as they last. But the shifting time frames
of the narrative also make clear that these classifications do not
last. They are the necessities of the moment, subject to change. A
constant series of differences that matter and that are always
changing are not differences of substance but of relation; differences become significant as the configuration of objects in a field
alters. No one particular position will provide purity, safety, or a
place from which to launch an attack. What *Zami* exemplifies is a
pluralist methodology in pursuit of consistent opposition.[24]

Lorde celebrates the outsider and her powers of insight and survival, but the outsider in *Zami* is always on the move. The structures of dominant culture are not (always) being abandoned, but
nor are they being uncritically embraced; rather Lorde takes the
available cultural formations and *moves in on* them. This is how,
for instance, Lorde refigures Audre's exclusion from the familial
structures of the Black community: she descends from making love
on a rooftop with Kitty, who is also sometimes and in some relations the goddess Afrekete, into Harlem:

> It was not onto the pale sands of Whydah, nor the beaches of Winneba
> or Annamabu, with cocopalms softly applauding and crickets keeping
> time with the pounding of a tar-laden, treacherous, beautiful sea. It
> was onto 113th Street that we descended after our meeting under the
> Midsummer Eve's Moon, but the mothers and fathers smiled at us in
> greeting as we strolled down to Eighth Avenue, hand in hand. (253)

This not-Africa is also not-Harlem, but a Harlem transfigured and
re-created by the imaginary intrusion. Audre comes into the family
as the child smiled upon by the Black community; this is a reconciliation with traditional terms (there are still mothers and fathers
here), but it is also something else, a challenge to the structure it
invades. In this scene, Audre's tactic is perhaps more assimilationist than anything; it is certainly more assimilationist than separatist. And yet if this is reconciliation, it is followed in the narrative by

the mythic escape to the other world of Carriacou (the place/strategy of Black Power?), and by Audre's successful completion of library school (the place/strategy of equal rights?). In *Zami* all the possible tactics for political opposition are played out, serially and together. It can be read, therefore, as a metatext of opposition, one that makes the fact of opposition important beyond the question of how it is done, or whether what one tactic achieves is consistent with the achievement of another. But the shifting of oppositional strategies according to what genre or what cultural formation one is faced with is a significant textual apparatus not because it happens in this one text, but because its exemplary existence is indicative of a more general cultural and hence critical possibility.[25]

"DON'T MYTHOLOGIZE ME": *A LITANY FOR SURVIVAL*

The Audre who issues out onto the streets of Black and white New York, the shape-changing scene-stealer, is a figure who believes in and acts upon her agency in the world. Her noisy presence will alter any field that she enters. The literal body enacts and authorizes the movement of the textual body; as Audre makes herself felt on fields of identity, forcing them to reconstitute around her otherness, so *Zami* and other Black lesbian and feminist texts moved in on canonical spaces, destabilizing and reconstituting the lines of literary transmission. Audre's journey into self-awareness in the '50s and '60s of "gay girl" bars, an awareness that is crucially that community's of her, parallels the entry of African-American women authors' works into a white-defined and -controlled canon of feminist literature in the '80s. Black feminist criticism then sought to identify and historicize a literary tradition, replacing absence with the recovered richness of transmission and influence, while at the same time white feminist ways of reading black women's texts began a steady shift away from the early impulse to marginalize toward that of colonization. The shift follows the change in prevailing versions of feminist theory. When it was still possible to universalize and promote a general category "woman" as unit of cultural and political identity and action, the marginal text, understood as reflecting and expressing the experience of its author's subject position, is read as adding richness to the portrait of a common experience of gender. What is important about it is generalizable; its specifics are de-emphasized. In this light, *The Women's Room* is a more "relevant" text than *Zami*. This theory's now obviously problematic erasure of marginal identity, of the racial category of whiteness, and of any other mechanisms of either oppression or taxonomy than gender, led to the fall of the universal woman, but it did not lead, despite its gestures in such a direction, to a fundamental revision of white feminist hegemony. The problem of the whiteness of discourse cannot, of course, be solved by the simple mechanism of changing the object of study.[26]

Nonetheless, critics have proceeded with this change, to the point where white reading increasingly privileges non-white texts over white ones. Where once the white feminist critic gestured more or less perfunctorily toward the black woman's text, this text now underpins her argument, has taken on the aura of the exemplary. As Elizabeth Abel has pointed out, the black text is a flexible counter, prayed in aid of diverse theoretical positions—for example, both grounding deconstruction and justifying its refutation. And as Valerie Smith remarked, commenting upon an early manifestation of this critical trend, this is a familiar position for the black body. The colonization of black texts by white critics is an overdetermined process, and has been explained variously as a response to the brilliance of the writing suddenly appearing and African-American writers' subsequent mainstream visibility, as an attempt to escape from the penalties of white feminist success into a form of textuality that both narratively and stylistically offers renewed possibilities for imagining resistance, and as a means to either rematerialize or justify a postmodern feminism in need of grounding on the body.[27] What does it mean that the white feminist project has come to depend upon the authorizing power of the black woman's text? From tokenistic inclusion to dependence is a large and troubling step, one that necessarily invokes a binary opposition between white absence and black presence. More troubling still is the remastering that white reading must represent, however carefully the critic disclaims the appropriative impulse at work in the interpretative act.

There is a scene in *Zami* where Muriel, Audre's white lover, draws up a list of her and Audre's accomplishments over the past year. Audre's half of the page is full (went back to school, wrote poems, and so on). On her own side, Muriel writes one word

"Nothing." From this moment, the writing is on Muriel's wall: she will slide further into depression and disease, while Audre moves onward and outward. The list is pivotal for both characters, not because the description invoked is an accurate one, but rather because it reveals, briefly, a point of view that Audre's narration largely occludes. Audre is surprised to find that Muriel thinks she's being so successful, for that isn't how it looks to her; and Muriel's self-description is for Audre a revelation of her hopelessness and an index of the necessity for separation. What Muriel has done is both to create and to define her own immobility by reference to Audre's activity, and to make her own sense of identity depend on that comparison. White is stuck; but also white is stuck because, as she constructs it, black is active. In the narrative context of *Zami*, Muriel's list is a guilt trip, one that Audre refuses to respond to. In the context of feminist criticism, Muriel's text is more appropriative than accusatory, but it equally depends upon the contrast between stasis and movement. Muriel's sickness is that she cannot emulate Audre's power; the white feminist critic has no such problem for, theoretically at least, to identify possibility is to inhabit it. While Muriel, in other words, is invested in restraining Audre, the white critic is invested in valorizing her resistant energy, the better to feed off it.

"I want the conjure woman," Jane Gallop says in *Around 1981: Academic Feminist Literary Theory* (1992) of her disappointment with the academic tone and apparatus of the African-American critical anthology edited by Marjorie Pryse and Hortense Spillers, *Conjuring: Black Women, Fiction, and Literary Tradition* (1985), remarking upon, and thus disavowing, her own investment in black folk authenticity, her desire for both the warm approving black mother and a cultural space of incontestable alterity.[28] Unsurprisingly, what she wants is what (she knows) she won't get: this desire will have to be deferred, redirected into the satisfactions of self-scrutiny. In place of acceptance within blackness, she will have to settle for analyzing why she wants to be there and for the distance from desire that such knowledge brings. Having suspicions as to the political valence of a desire, being elegantly self-reflexive about one's theoretical practice: these are admirable qualities in criticism. But what, ultimately, should be the relation between white feminist critic and black text?[29]

Gallop's self-reflexivity is now a familiar process, directed toward both earlier incarnations of the writer's own critical practice and those of others: rather than just write about white women writers or black women writers, white critics write about other white critics and their appropriation of texts of color. Margaret Homans excoriates Judith Butler and Donna Haraway for their use of women of color's textual strategies as alibis for their deconstructive theoretical projects, taking up the analysis made by Morrison and Valerie Smith of a critical and cultural practice whereby blackness figures as embodiment, the ground of experience for the theoretical edifice of the white mind. Elizabeth Abel in "Black Writing, White Reading," critiques Barbara Johnson and Homans, and her own reading of Morrison, arguing that both the limitation and the justification for white on black reading is the inexorable failure of identification between the two, that they thus work to render whiteness visible. And here I am, one more white feminist adding another layer of refraction to these receding mirrorings. It is not hard to metaphorize this situation—perhaps as a pack of jackals worrying a carcass—but the anxious white feminists' enquiry into our own obsession with racially marked texts is not so simply an act of domination and victimization. To present it thus would be to repeat the move that has now been defamiliarized from all angles, presenting the black woman/text as the body upon which/from which others operate, figuring the black text as innocence and purity, the sign of otherness so fervently the object of white desire.[30]

The question of consumption, of who is consumed by whom in the restless reading and rereading that is current feminist critical practice, is complicated. And the relation between critic and text is shifty, too. The "conjure woman" is an active agent, one whose ways of knowing may not be so easily pinned down by theoretical practice. It is not necessarily the case that her invocation in white feminists' accounts of difference enacted, otherness articulated, repeats, *tout court,* the cannibal's appropriation of his vanquished foe's courage. Who controls the critical text if its figuration of disruption must be cast in the conjure woman's terms, and what has she to say of this passionate attention?

I want to read *A Litany for Survival* in the light of the various positionings suggested both by the triumphal oppositionality of *Zami* and by the situation of the Black text and the black body in relation to its institutional reading in various cultural contexts.

The later text continues *Zami* in various ways, but it is also a radical revision, speaking to different audiences and producing an alternative model of resistance, one that is constructed in the light of the critical history of the years between *Zami* and *Litany*. This reading is thus both of texts in relation and of texts in relation to their audiences: it seeks to produce *Litany* as a film that simultaneously challenges and reinscribes modes of resistance, and also to pay attention to how the film addresses a range of audiences and constituencies. As part of the latter consideration, I will return to the problem of one of those potential audiences, the white feminist.

Because *Litany* is a film about Lorde made by others, it obviously constructs Lorde as a text in a different way than does the self-authorizing biomythography, but the distinction is less absolute than it seems, given the weight placed on Lorde's own words and her authoritative presence. The film is largely made up of interviews with Lorde, interviews with her peers, friends, and family, and clips of Lorde at readings or giving classes and speeches. Apart from some home-movie style footage of Lorde at home, she is usually declaiming directly to the camera. The filmmakers' vision, while clearly present in the juxtaposition of interviews about Lorde with her own words, barely seems to constrain Lorde's control of the medium or her capacity for self-presentation on her own terms. Partly this is a function of the film's respectful tone, its mission to eulogize the dying poet-activist, in addition to her mentoring position toward both the filmmakers and many of the audiences she is depicted addressing; it also derives from the fact that most of the words spoken, whether as voiceover, taped speech, interview, or extract from published work, are Lorde's own. The film, by virtue of its construction, is much more dialogic than *Zami*, where narrative control is synonymous with self-determination, but ultimately it is not the various versions of Lorde that are put into conversation with one another: the important conversation is the one that Lorde is having with her audience(s).

Houston Baker's claim that the African-American critical project is most radical when occupying autobiographical space is complicated where the resisting subject is female, as Mae Henderson points out, by the specular possibilities offered by the black woman as image.[31] To this problem must be added that of the effect of individual life cycles upon the autobiographical act which is also self-consciously a political one. Between the publication of *Zami* and the making of *Litany*, Lorde became representative of opposition, her writing used as exemplary of antihegemonic ways of reimagining identity and political structures, her person a figure for a complex, resistant way of being. The kind of fame Lorde attained can be distinguished from, for instance, Toni Morrison's; Morrison functions to represent contemporary African-American literature and its continued assertion of difference from versions of white reality, and her work is also mined by feminist criticism, but Lorde represents resistance in her own person—this is what she is famous for, what all the words that attach to "Audre Lorde" refer back to; Lorde *is* the "Sister Outsider" she articulated as a political position. The persona of *Zami* exemplifies this figuration, that of the being in struggle. The arena may change, the local circumstances vary, but the struggle, and Audre's engagement in it, is constant.

This positionality intersects, one might say, with the process and development of an individual life, but certain tensions exist and expand as the person who operates from within the iconic structure moves away from it. Icons, of course, are immortal, unlike the bodies that accommodate their meaning. One of the questions that *Litany* must negotiate as *Zami*—the account of a young woman's search for self—need not is Lorde's failure to survive. How is the death of the individual to be accommodated and acknowledged without negating the figurative survival that the icon expects, or that we confer upon it? The film presents this difficulty visually, for the camera captures Lorde at various stages of her long fight with cancer, a losing battle that is depicted through the slow shedding of flesh and strength from one clip to another. While the process of the disease is not rendered, as the life is not rendered, chronologically, the inevitability of the endpoint is established at the outset both by a clip of Lorde, obviously weak, struggling to record the sky on a camcorder as if she does not expect to see it again, and by her valedictory opening voiceover: "What I leave behind . . ."[32] The nonchronological editing operates to reinforce the constant presence of Lorde's cancer and its terminal nature, since an image of Lorde in apparent health is repeatedly juxtaposed with another where sickness is evident, requiring that the viewer always read the life through the encroaching death. The film can of course seek to celebrate a life, but how is it to celebrate survival, as both *Zami* and *The Cancer Journals* (1980) do? The obvious move here is to memorialize the enduring legacy of Lorde's work, invoking a poignant but not unexpected contrast between immortality of word and mortality of flesh. I want to argue, however, that something other is going on in *Litany*, that, in fact, Lorde is arguing for the nonsurvival of her iconic presence, for a refusal of the stasis that a legacy inevitably brings.

As a medium, film must render Lorde more literally visible at the same time that it gives her less control over the projected image and how it is used. Self-definition is less absolute, for in the move between Audre as narrator and Lorde as iconic object there have been two shifts of agency. Lorde no longer authors herself, instead giving over production to the filmmakers who fashion her life; but in addition the viewer is in a different relation to the film than is the reader to the written "biomythography." Lorde dies—off camera, but none the less inevitably. When she intones, a skeletal talking head, the poem "This Is Not the Day," the assertion of death's absence on that particular day gains its power in part from the fragility of such an assertion from a dying mouth, as well as from its continued denial. Death is denied by, perhaps, a few days: while it is an heroic gesture, it is also a small and markedly temporary one. Lorde's defiant search for a way to defeat and stave off cancer is constantly mediated for the viewer by the image of her close to death. This personal loss, the impossibility of holding the self intact, away from dissolution, is repeated in the public register, and it is this repetition in another order of meaning that lends *Litany* its significance as a text of a different form of resistance. By deconstructing her own iconic image, Lorde is able to suggest the limitations of icon formation as a form of cultural process while at the same time hinting that the failure finally to exemplify success—or successful resistance—is in itself an act of opposition.

The film puts in motion a dialectic between Lorde as iconic survivor and the gradual failing of the flesh. This movement—the undermining movement—depends upon the possibility and consistency of a slippage between the actual, individual body and the body as signifier. For what Lorde is most iconically an embodiment of is survival itself. "We were never meant to survive," she intones in voiceover, and whereas *Zami, The Cancer Journals,* and *A Burst of Light* are accounts of survival against the institutional and personal odds, *Litany* is not. In *Zami*, Lorde mythifies herself, endowing Audre as protagonist with meaning beyond her individual struggle. The autobiographical self is rewritten so that it is always added to, can never be accessed before textualization. In her writings about cancer and cancer treatment Lorde writes autobiographically, but her body becomes exemplary of cultural invasion. In refusing the pink prosthesis that a racist hospital administration would seek to place upon her body in place of the amputated black breast, Lorde figures the situation of many marginal subjectivities, as well as the operations of contemporary femininity upon the black female body. In *Litany*, however, it is the existence of two bodies and the difference between them that is constantly present to the viewer. The vibrancy and power of the iconic figure, she whose strength is infinite and multifaceted, points up the frailty of the physical body: the body, that is, to which Lorde is finally reduced. The film follows Lorde into public and private, and as a result the domestic sphere is never entirely that alone. Yet the private body is finally the one that controls the most apparently public and iconic representations. The film invites us to see the skeleton beneath the monument's surface. The iconic image cracks; the poet finally loses her voice—on which, she tells the camera hoarsely, she had always relied in order to be able to hear her poems internally. It is in a new breathy, rasping tone that she reads "Today Is Not the Day." Behind the image of Lorde's capacity to confront her death in the poem, to the camera, lies the inevitable end of the struggle. The struggle against death is in the context of Lorde's body of work the struggle against cancer, against a hostile world which promotes and enables high cancer rates among black women; it is the struggle against a racist, homophobic world that seeks to extinguish difficult Black lesbians. And in dying, visibly, Lorde acknowledges the failure of that struggle—the struggle that Audre fought for an identity seized. Her visibility becomes visibility as failure as well as success. Visibility itself turns from triumphant self-assertion into self-exposure; it rewrites visibility *as* self-exposure. This is a deliberate exposure of self: for in so revealing the skeleton, Lorde the shape-changer, she of many strategies, shows how large is the enemy, how impossible the fight that must be fought, how limited resistance must always be, and how mobile. In throwing oneself against the wall, one renders it peculiarly present to the gaze; but the wall is thus illuminated as too high to climb, too solid to penetrate.

Resisting Audiences

The first action that we see Lorde performing in the film's history of the production of the artifact of herself ("What I leave behind has a life of its own. I've said this about poetry. I'm saying it
about the artifact of who I have been.") is her acceptance of the
appointment as "New York State Poet." Governor Cuomo, bestow-
ing the honor, confers the "Walt Whitman Citation of Merit for
Poets." In the aftermath of this fascinating refiguring of the American literary canon, Lorde goes on to give a speech in the tradition
of American dissent. What does it mean, Lorde asks, that she,
"Black Lesbian feminist warrior poet mother," should be acquiring
this status in a context of the continued and systematic exploitation
and oppression practiced in and by the same institution that is
honoring her? It means, she answers herself, "that we live in a
world full of the most intense contradiction." The speech's position
at the beginning of the film might suggest that Lorde has taken up
the "master's tools" which she famously repudiated at an earlier
moment, the better to dismantle the master's house.[33] But Lorde's
jeremiad turns out to be a false trail, or at least the road not taken,
for this is the only time in the film that she appears in such a context, resisting appropriation by the official public sphere, operating within a hegemonic institution as an agent of contestation.

The narrative of herself, and of resistance to appropriation, is
focused elsewhere. Many other public events feature in the film,
but they are public events in a series of counter-public spheres:
there are long extracts from a conference organized by African-
American women to honor Lorde, at which we hear Lorde, a
South African political activist, and several younger African-American poets. There are flashes of Lorde teaching a poetry workshop
and of her leading a seminar for Afro-Germans. Apart from the
domestic footage of Lorde at home in St. Croix, Lorde's personal
history is also a counter-public sphere production, provided by a
voiceover that reads extracts from *Zami* against a collage of black
and white newsclips and photographs of the 1950s and '60s.

The film produces a series of narratives that engender, in turn,
a series of positionings in the white feminist critic watching. That
process of engagement itself promotes and constructs other narratives, elaborations based in watching from a distance/difference.

The first narrative is that of Lorde as Mother Poet, inspiration, model, scourge, and resource for a younger generation of African-American writers. In the creative writing class, we hear her exhorting her class to search within for what they have to say; Sapphire, in her interview, locates Lorde as central to her poetic vocation; even Sonia Sanchez, recounting that at one time she hadn't wanted to read with Lorde because of Lorde's assertion of her sexuality, places herself in the relation of one who has learned to listen to Lorde's wisdom. Jewelle Gomez articulates neatly the dialectic around which Lorde's cultural construction turns: "There are some of us who think of Audre—we never say this out loud—but we think of Audre as, um, *mother*" [original emphasis]. The film gives us Lorde as artistic, activist icon in the African-American community. When Gloria Joseph, Lorde's lover in the present of the film, protests "I did not meet Audre as this great big Black goddess to be idealized—I met her, you know, I would say on an equal footing," the deification is almost complete. Joseph's remark is closely followed by Lorde's own resistance to her placement. Because the film is edited so that we hear Lorde in voiceover before we see that she is addressing a class of student poets, these words seem directed to a much wider audience: "You have *got* to go on [overriding protests]. [Y]ou *don't* need me, don't you understand, the me that you're talking about you carry around inside *yourselves*. . . . [Y]ou can do it for yourselves. . . . Don't *mythologize* me" (original emphasis). At the moment of repudiating her myth, Lorde also reinforces it: she will be the internalized progenitor, the new poets' voices growing out of her presence within.

I must work to position myself in relation to this narrative because it explicitly does not seek to include the white viewer. These are (almost all) African-American women (and a few men) talking to each other about a shared cultural phenomenon; nothing suggests that the appropriate stance here is to identify right along with, cheerfully crossing racial difference to empathize with the importance of Lorde to all our artistic and political developments. My viewing position is decentered; I am placed at the distance that comes from listening to a conversation in which one is interested but does not expect to be included. There are many occasions on which Lorde chose to speak to particular communities, and this aspect of the film re-creates that strategy, both enacting it and pointing to it; because the separatism is enfolded within a film that as a whole encompasses a wider audience, it is both more and less itself—more separatist because the gesture is seen by all, and less so because, after all, we are all allowed to listen, whoever we are, even while we cannot effortlessly participate.[34] But it is not so easy to listen to the words of the goddess mother, watching as her legacy is passed down, without wanting to be included, without feeling rejected by this supreme and caring deity. A schematic moment in the film brings my own desire for inclusion to the surface. Lorde speaks (initially, it is not clear to whom) of the political work that can and must be done across difference; "I don't have to *be* you in order to work with you" [original emphasis], and I find myself pleased and grateful—emotions embarrassingly clarified by the disappointment induced by the next sentence: "I don't have to be you to respect your Blackness." These two moments—Lorde's acceptance of her internalization by the aspiring poets and her articulation of the possibility of coalition across (unspecified) difference—exemplify and enact models of relation to which the white viewer is not given access. The film performs and manifests an exclusion, requiring that this viewer be rendered conscious of her (dis)identifications.

This is not the only narrative that declines to speak directly to a white audience and, largely, to speak of it. The most obvious gap in the film's historical account is the absence of Lorde's (white) ex-husband: a picture of him, wheeling a push-chair, features briefly, but he is not interviewed. This is an absence that repeats the selectivity of the story Lorde chooses to tell in *Zami*, where the narrative closes with the celebratory Africanized sensual encounter with Afrekete, leaving Lorde's interracial, heterosexual interlude quietly in the unspoken future. In the film, Lorde mentions her marriage, and the snapshot of a father in action is sufficient to alert the viewer to his suppression from the rich weaving of story, reminiscence, and anecdote; so *A Litany for Survival* repeats *Zami*'s practice of exclusion, but with a difference. Respecting Lorde's wish that he not be interviewed, the filmmakers nonetheless gesture toward including and acknowledging him in the history they are constructing, just as they circulate the film to wider audiences. And this has a double effect: *Litany* renders visible the exclusion that *Zami* merely performs.[35]

White feminism's engagement with Lorde is represented in the film by Adrienne Rich, who mourns the loss of Lorde particularly as fellow-poet, the irreplaceable one with whom her work could be shared, discussed, worked over. Although Rich's meaning for the film's audience encompasses her position as lesbian feminist activist and writer, in other words, her contribution is not from that positionality but from a much more intimate and personal place of poetic connection. Rich's artistic identity can and has outweighed her whiteness: Lorde and the filmmakers speak to the poet. But the tone of Rich's interview is suggestively different from that of many others. While Lorde's disciples and friends are celebratory and upbeat, Rich seems close to tears. She speaks of Lorde in the past tense, as if she were already dead. Literally, the collaborative communication between the two poets presumably ended with Lorde's move to St. Croix, but perhaps the temporal dislocation of Rich's perception also reflects her sense of Lorde's having withdrawn from engagement across racial difference. If Lorde speaks from within the next generation of poets of color, Rich's valediction can imagine no such legacy for white ones.

As I have noted, Lorde's only current and visible act of engagement with whiteness in the film is the clip of her accepting the New York State Poet award in a speech in which Lorde notes her contradictory position in relation to this public sphere, the cultural arm of the military-industrial complex.[36] Since the granting of the accolade New York State Poet is made to stand for Lorde's fame—and her attitude toward that fame—in the "white world," it is inviting to read its significance in terms of metonymy rather than metaphor: whatever this honor means, so success in dominant culture means. It would be hard to imagine a more meaningless accolade, one more empty of affect or power. It is insultingly obvious that North American states endow their designated poet with about as much political power as is granted the official state bird. Neither is expected to be other than ornamental; the state apparatus functions very efficiently without the engagement of either birds or poems, although occasionally one may wish to paint one on a bomber or engrave something inspiring on a public building in order to arouse a little patriotic sentiment.

Are the exhaustive acclamations and appropriations of Lorde by white feminists, including my own, as alien and politically irrelevant—except insofar as they might provide a platform for a repudiating speech—as New York State? If we take the film's stance seriously, is white feminists' ceaseless invocation of Lorde's "house of difference" on a par with poems on bombs? In pondering this question it seems relevant that Lorde could always be relied upon to be angry when appropriated; she could be bothered, most of the time, to tell white women off, and this was reassuring—it showed that we mattered and she still cared. Speaking to many audiences in many public forums, Lorde regularly took advantage of her position at the podium to say what white listeners, in particular, didn't much want to hear. Sometimes she would tell an eager white lesbian crowd to please stop listening and leave, because there were black women who needed our seats more.[37] Sometimes, accepting an award, she would use her acceptance speech to remark upon the tokenism that such an honor represented, and admonish the judges to come back next year with evidence of having made substantial changes in their practice, rather than empty gestures of which she was the recipient.[38] And it is Lorde's own restless return to engagement even with some unpromising audiences that partly authorizes some version of this continuing process. But what version?[39]

A final narrative layer: *A Litany for Survival* is made over a period of years, and in it Lorde appears at various stages of relative health and sickness, but while the narrative moves backwards and forwards chronologically, there is no escaping the overarching teleology of the progress of the cancer that Lorde fights and lives with throughout. The attention to Lorde's disease is authorized both, presumably, by Lorde herself and by *The Cancer Journals* and *A Burst of Light*, where the personal narrative of sickness mediates Lorde's engagement with the politics of disease and its management. Between *The Cancer Journals* and *A Burst of Light* breast cancer metastasizes into liver cancer; a disease we are encouraged to believe we can "overcome" reemerges as one that is figured as inexorably terminal. The reigning discourse in women's health circles inscribes breast cancer as an epidemic, and as an epidemic whose seriousness has been occluded by the patriarchal medical establishment.[40] Lorde's death thus is enacted within another feminist rhetorical frame: she is dying of the disease of which women die because of systemic neglect.

This politicized reading of Lorde's illness requires that the white feminist viewer see in Lorde's progress into death an anticipation not only of her own more or less imminent mortality but also of her own specifically female endangerment: having breasts in a masculist culture is a potentially terminal affliction in itself. Here, finally, is a position of identification that the film apparently invites. But breast cancer is no equal opportunity disease: death rates are higher for African-American than for white American women. Identifying on the basis of gender is thus, to say the least, complicated by race as the healthy white feminist watches the Black warrior poet die. We must wonder whether we can watch this death and not commodify it. One resolution to this particular impasse is Friedman's in " 'Beyond' Gynocriticism and Gynesis"; by invoking "relational positionality"—the simultaneous existence of many axes of identity—Friedman is able to read a matrix of shifting power relations without any one particular identity or position obliterating others. Friedman's elegant taxonomy elucidates with exemplary clarity the web of crossings, alliances, and changing relations that make up the individual subject's experience of the social. It allows the common identity of twentieth-century American women as vulnerable to breast cancer to coexist with the axis on which whiteness confers privilege within the medical system. It allows for both identification and difference, exclusion and inclusion. But despite the persuasiveness of this methodology, and its power to anatomize complex representations, something more seems necessary to accommodate the desire and discomfort that such shifting and overlayering of boundaries evoke. How, as I weep through the closing credits of *Litany*, is this not to become another enactment of sentiment, which both requires an imaginary sameness and erases the crucial differences of social power?

The problem with a model that is based in multiple shifting identities as a way of both understanding and representing power relations is that it can take insufficient account of how power is reconfigured in the act of reading. Lorde produces herself as icon of resistance, but in very specific locations. She also, as I suggested earlier, points to the limitations of any resistance that becomes iconic, while at the same time reinscribing the act of resistance itself as a necessary gesture. The act of identification departicularizes the local, at the same time as it tends to solidify resistance into its most iconic form as a transferable essence. *A Litany for Survival* works to structure and define difference between audiences, which are also differences in power relations. But only in the act of scripting the film, and in its enactment of Lorde's performative speeches, does power to define, to address or not, remain with directors or protagonist rather than with the viewer. And what we see in the film is the black body as resistance, but also the black body in resistance, working against the readings of its audiences.

This is not an argument against reading across difference. But I would propose that the reading of Lorde, and the invocation of her oppositional strategies, must proceed in the recognition of the inappropriateness and nonavailability of sameness and identification. If we take Lorde and her marking of difference seriously, then it behooves white feminist critics to resist their own desire to belong in Audre's house. The use of Lorde by white feminism, in other words, should be understood as a move into coalition—and coalition is a limited engagement. Bernice Johnson Reagon's much cited call for political alliance in "Coalition Politics" contains a crucial caveat about what coalitions can do, and where they happen. This less celebrated aspect of Johnson's argument bears upon the current problem, for she draws a distinction between "home" on the one hand and the place of coalition on the other. The latter is unpleasant, uncomfortable, difficult, and bruising—which is why, in part, one has need of home, the place of sameness, where the coalition builder withdraws for nurture, understanding, and re-plenishment. As *Litany* makes clear, Lorde does not say the same things to different audiences, and the many selves that seek to control the discourse in their different appearances do not operate the same way out of context. In the public space of coalition, the house of difference, Lorde embodies resistance to as much as resistance for; the doubling of that position allows for the desiring critic's act, but acknowledges her object's resistance, and the value, and social reality of that difference.

Afterword

Successful instrumental texts may tell us less than we think: whatever the extent of *Uncle Tom's Cabin*'s influence on the Civil War, it is hard to imagine using Stowe's text as a blueprint for the politically engaged work. Its mechanisms, from this historical distance, seem both dubious and opaque; even if sentiment still seemed an acceptable route to shifting public opinion in a progressive direction, the novel's incapacity to imagine a livable alternative world without the racism it both excoriates and inhabits seems disqualifying. Nonetheless *Uncle Tom's Cabin*'s apparent success, exactly because of this, does tell us something: that its effect hung upon the conditions of its original reception, upon the ways in which in that particular context it could be put to use.

I have been arguing here that cultural interventions that have become embedded in reception history and story as successes are in fact, insofar as their political effect is concerned, failures: Wollstonecraft's words served only to solidify, motivate, and justify a profoundly reactionary, misogynist public discourse; *The Women's Room* advanced the cause of individualism, if that; *The Accused*'s solution to social injustice reinscribed the inevitability of sadistic means to knowledge and power. What is particular about these failures is the persistence of the success story that hangs about them. Success invites replication; nobody wants to repeat failure. Contingency works upon failure as well as success, but with the latter there is a ready aura of the replaceable, of possible iterability. These are failures that have successfully disguised themselves as successes: on the level of cultural narrative, that is, they have indeed succeeded. Both aspects are informative: read as failures, they reveal the solidity of dominant discourse, its infinitely resourceful capacity to read resistance back into acquiescence, its drive toward containment. They show how little the instrumental text can do. And read as successes, they illuminate the critical will to find the instrumental text, the shining sword of oppositional

128

discourse waiting to be released from its embedding rock. The successful instrumental text, after all, is a powerful source of meaning and motivation. The dream of agency is hard to abandon, and even in questioning it, its continued currency seems politically necessary. The belief in the instrumental text has served feminist purposes, providing a narrative of the continued possibility of social change, organizing past and future, creating and preserving a link between activism and academia. But it is time, I think, to move on from this happy faith. The nostalgic recycling of consciousness-raising texts has held a section of feminist criticism back from looking for new strategies for changing circumstances as well as from reevaluating old ones. That reading was action once should not be the basis for a static model either for engagement with the text or for political engagement itself. The tendency of the feminist critic has been to overprivilege the text, granting it a kind of originary status, as of the beacon that spreads the chain of enlightenment. But the extreme fallibility of the instrumental text suggests to me a rather different metaphor: the instrumental text as the string of fairy lights that remains stubbornly darkened if only one bulb in the chain is faulty or not quite connected, that when it comes flickeringly to life is at the mercy of any mechanical failure or the slightest earthborne breeze. Such fragility requires an intensity of focus on context; to historicize in the light of a theory of the instrumental text that can so fitfully shed its own must be to search out in depth and detail and texture the web that supported that transient agent for its brief tenure.

The possibility that the feminist book that changes women's lives is more cultural fiction than history, that it works as originary myth of feminist agency, rather than dogma, can have positive, if unsettling, consequences. The fallibility of the instrumental text has implications for feminist canon formation, and in particular for that canon in action in the women's studies classroom. Canons are constructed for many reasons, of course, most of which do not depend upon instrumentality; but nonetheless many texts canonized on the syllabus are prized in part because of their supposed capacity to enable or incite feminist literacy in the reader. If the statement "This book changed my life" were no longer immediately legible as implying "and, if you learn to read it the right way, it can change yours," a series of pedagogical and perhaps critical expectations must alter. When the first sentence itself no longer invokes immediate assent, but seems instead a perilous assertion; when it would have to be acknowledged as having a much more complicated, tentative, and historically inflected grammar; then the ground for reading starts to shift in interesting ways. No one who has taught the same text to two different but apparently demographically identical groups of people needs to be told that reading scenes, and the effects manifested there, are variable and unpredictable; in the women's studies classroom, where raising the consciousness of the audience is, whether more or less overtly, part of both agenda and expectation, this variation can be critical. To know that there is no feminist magic bullet that can alter ways of seeing and knowing, and to know this critically and theoretically as it is known in practice, requires that we motivate and present texts otherwise. One might, in this altered critical context, still read *The Women's Room*, or *The Golden Notebook*. But it would be much less compelling, as a reading method, to disconnect formal structure—the apparently permanent skeleton of the textual—from the whispering, nebulous miasma of cultural contingency. It would be necessary, too, to investigate the possible impermanence of form; how form itself might be differently animated, differently textured within a reading scene that triggers, that molds, that compresses in fleeting ways.

A loss of faith in the instrumental text is also of course necessarily an admission of some loss of faith in texts. We cannot accommodate the limitations of texts as instruments of social change unless we also acknowledge that other forms of action are usually more effective. Conversely, I think that we also need to think otherwise about failure and its potential. Of course there has always been a certain power granted the heroic failure, but this is a different gesture, one that is not grand but that makes what it can of materials available to hand. *Thelma and Louise* is a current example; the film's ending could itself be construed as an heroic failure, given that the heroes drive decisively off a cliff to their deaths, but the film's *use*, the way it has been put into play in the public sphere, has involved gestures of a different kind. The stubborn dystopian element—the lack of an imaginable place or way of survival—that the dead-end leap encodes is crucial to the film's power, to its effectiveness in feminist redeployments. (One might notice that this is in its own right a gesture that, quiet suicide apart, is not routinely available to the female entrapped: "She had nowhere else to go," Humbert

remarks as Lolita turns weeping into his embrace.[1]) However, the
bumper sticker that declares "Thelma and Louise Live!" rewrites
the textual self-annihilation, making of the characters' death something else: an assertion of resistance.[2] Audre Lorde's simultaneous
reassertion and deconstruction of the resistant "I," of the identity
in resistance that is the project of *Zami*, has functioned here as my
exemplary text of failure, for it self-consciously moves away from
all the fixities that seem to signal success, agency, and power—
away from visibility. *Litany for Survival* is not in any simple sense
about failure, any more than the film itself fails in its celebratory
and memorializing program. Only in the context of *Zami* and of
Lorde's status as icon of opposition does the film's enactment
of death and survival become legible as a claim not for the survival of
a figurehead, a myth, or even a legacy—the manifest content
of what Lorde and the filmmakers pass on—but for survival of
opposition itself, by any means necessary.

Notes

INTRODUCTION: THE USE OF BLUNT INSTRUMENTS

1. See Judith Fetterley, *The Resisting Reader*; but the phrase encapsulates an enduring element in feminist criticism, since our origin story is of opposition to a primordial, exclusionary symbolic and social order.

2. The value of that activist past, and the nature of various critics' relation to it, are contentious issues, particularly since theoretical and political disagreements have begun to be expressed in generational terms. But my point here is that, irrespective of her position in that debate, a feminist critic will have some position in relation to the past of the women's liberation movement, even if it is one of repudiation.

3. For an extended discussion of the history of "causal mimesis" as a reading practice, particularly as it relates to the reception of *Huckleberry Finn*, see Steven Mailloux, "Cultural History and *Huckleberry Finn*," *Rhetorical Power*, 57–129.

4. An example of this belief in institutional operation was the 1990 Modern Language Association panel chaired by Florence Howe, "Books That Changed Our Lives," at which feminist critics reminisced about which text transformed their own life, the tenor of the occasion clearly being that individual change of this sort had larger, political, significance; that this is a specifically feminist form of institutionalized faith is suggested by the absence of comparable panels at which marxian critics or deconstructionists gather to perform similar acts of memory. (Although feminist critics who are also either of these might well do so in the appropriate feminist context.)

5. In addition to those from which I quote here, some examples are Patricia Duncker, *Sisters and Strangers*, Molly Hite, *The Other Side of the Story*, Roberta Rubenstein, *Boundaries of the Self*, Lorna Sage, *Women in the House of Fiction*, and Patricia Waugh, *Feminine Fictions*.

6. Marie Lauret, *Liberating Literature*, viii. Lauret's account of feminist fiction is careful, persuasive, and thorough; it is unusual both in paying as much attention to the texts of nonwhite authors as it does to what have become, in feminist accounts of movement and movement-associated fiction, the usual white suspects, and in situating second-wave feminism and its literary production within the context of the civil rights movement and the New Left. Lauret does what she sets out to do brilliantly; but she ignores the particular issue in which I am interested.

7. Gayle Greene, *Changing the Story*, 56–57. Greene presents the story of feminist fiction as one of rise to instrumental power and subsequent fall into "postfeminism"; in her view, the problem is that books used to change lives, but don't seem to any more.

8. As Rose notes, Joanne S. Frye is exemplary of the search for a revolutionary form, claiming in *Living Stories* both that the woman reader "participates in the feminist alteration of human experience," 191, and that "to alter literary form is to participate in the process of altering women's lives," 33.

Not all critics writing about contemporary women's fiction are concerned with the paradigmatic book that changes a life; Rachel Blau DuPlessis's *Writing Beyond the Ending* is just one example of the excellent work done in the field without reference to this question.

9. Rose proposes as an alternative the "common reader," who reads "to find reflections, confirmations, and clarifications of the problems [she] confront[s] daily," 347. This definition itself encodes some universal assumptions, of which Rose is not unaware. See Carey Kaplan and Rose, eds., *The Canon and the Common Reader*.

10. Cora Kaplan, "Feminist Criticism," 18.

11. Susannah Radstone has argued against the power of such texts to catalyze either individual or social change, questioning the myth of individual agency which emerges in women's movement stories of self-fashioning, and suggesting that readers attach the fact of change to the experience of reading rather than consider that alterations in social consciousness may be directed from without and may, furthermore, "form part of a shift from one femininity to another, with our lives forming part of a transition which, given the benefit of a wider historical perspective, we might neither welcome nor . . . celebrate," "Introduction: Sweet Dreams and the Perverse Imagination," 12.

12. The term "high renaissance" is originally from Rose; Hogeland deploys it with some irony. Hogeland divides consciousness-raising into two types, "hard" and "soft," which she defines, respectively, as "theory-building" and "promoting self-esteem"; by the terms of these definitions, the consciousness-raising novels she discusses are "soft."

13. Hogeland, *Feminism and Its Fictions*, 12–13.

14. It is also consistent with second-wave feminism's belief in the revolutionary power of the word. For commentary on this phenomenon, see, for example, Jan Clausen, "A Movement of Poets," Sara Maitland, "Futures in Feminist Fiction," and Patricia Waugh, *Metafiction*.

15. Tania Modleski's critique of Hitchcock in *The Woman Who Knew Too Much* makes a reverse form of this argument, proposing that Hitchcock's films can be consciousness-raising because of their antifeminism (the reader is goaded into consciousness), but she is arguing only for the possible effect on individual readers and viewers, rather than for Hitchcock as potentially an agent of progressive social change.

16. Susan Gubar's "What Ails Feminist Criticism?" is a recent, and prominent, defense of gender-privileging as feminist critical methodology; her targets, apart from postmodernism, Gayatri Chakravorty Spivak as representative of postcolonial studies, and Judith Butler as deconstruction's bad performative girl, also include Susan Stanford Friedman, who proposes decentering gender in " 'Beyond' Gynocriticism and Gynesis." See also Robyn Wiegman's ascerbic response, "What Ails Feminist Criticism: A Second Opinion," and Gubar's equally ascerbic reply, "Notations in Media Res."

17. It could be argued that my study preserves a framework—a study of white-authored work that includes a token nonwhite text—that Robyn Wiegman in *American Anatomies* critiques for failing to address race privilege. For an extended discussion of the problem of my own and other white critics' use of racially marked texts, see chapter 4. There have, of course, been many instrumental texts by nonwhite authors (an earlier version of this study included a chapter on Harriet Jacobs's *Incidents in the Life of a Slave Girl* [1861]); the white-authored texts are focused on here because my interest is particularly in how oppositional work gets read and assimilated into mainstream culture, and in reconsidering those texts that feminist criticism has most celebrated.

18. The encounter between feminism and postmodernism is systematically staged in Linda J. Nicholson, ed., *Feminism/Postmodernism;* for rather more postmodern leaning variants, see Jennifer Wicke and Margaret Ferguson, eds., *Feminism and Postmodernism,* Seyla Benhabib, *Situating the Self,* and Diane Elam, *Feminism and Deconstruction.* For postmodernism's repudiation, see, for example, Barbara Christian, "The Race for Theory." For an extended debate on the question of agency, see Judith Kegan Gardiner, ed., *Provoking Agents.*

19. See Teresa de Lauretis, "Eccentric Subjects," 144.

20. For postcolonial critiques of identity and the construction of the hybrid, see, for example, Homi K. Bhabha, "Interrogating Identity: The Postcolonial Prerogative," and Bhabha, ed., *Nation and Narration.* For an early intervention decentering gender, see Cherríe Moraga and Gloria Anzaldúa, eds., *This Bridge Called My Back.* For an example of a critique of white feminist colonialist practice, see Chandra Talpade Mohanty, "Under Western Eyes: Feminist Scholarship and Colonial Discourses." For an attempt to render multiplicity and contradiction as tools for politically progressive reading, see Friedman, " 'Beyond' Gynocriticism and Gynesis."

21. Elizabeth Wilson, "Tell It Like It Is," 32–33.

22. Lauren Berlant, "The Female Complaint," 243.

23. Rita Felski, *Beyond Feminist Aesthetics,* 9.

24. See Raymond Williams, "Structures of Feeling," in *Marxism and Literature,* 128–35.

25. The term "marginal" has come under some pressure, in the sense in which I use it here, that is, to designate a subject position other than the normative; however, because of the way in which the formulation margin/center repeats a binary opposition which it seeks to disrupt, I am retaining it, while acknowledging the difficulty, because of the accuracy with which the binary structure describes the process of opposition.

26. Sue-Ellen Case's essay "Toward a Butch-Feminist Retro-Future" gives an extended version of this point, lamenting, among other threatened counter-public sphere formations, the loss of noncapitalist forms of economic organizing: "What was once a lesbian or gay community is now becoming a market sector," 212.

27. See Chéla Sandoval, "U.S. Third World Feminism," and "Feminist Forms of Agency and Oppositional Consciousness," for two formulations of Sandoval's ideas.

28. For an example of such a conjunction of circumstances, see my "Death and

the Mainstream: Lesbian Detective Fiction and the Killing of the Coming-Out Story."

Chapter 1. Mary Wollstonecraft, or the Politics of Being Read

1. Mary Wollstonecraft, *A Vindication of the Rights of Woman*, 309. Subsequent quotations from this work are cited parenthetically in the text.

2. The "mere autobiography" and the "retreat from controversy" readings have been favored by Wollstonecraft's biographers; see below. Mary Poovey indicts Wollstonecraft in *The Proper Lady and the Woman Writer* for shifting, in the move from *Rights of Woman* to *Wrongs of Woman*, into a feminine and hence both sexualized and sentimentalized discourse, while Mary Jacobus claims in *Reading Woman* that the way of knowing occupied by Wollstonecraft in the later work is a potentially radical shift into feminine *différance*.

3. For an account of the shifting meanings and political uses to which the concept of "republican womanhood" was put in the early years of the Revolution, see Joan Landes, *Women and the Public Sphere in the Age of the French Revolution*. Wollstonecraft's argument in *Rights* is formulated not only within the constraints of the concept of republican womanhood but also in the light of present female degeneracy. While her aim in *Rights of Woman* is to extend Paine's doctrine of natural rights to female citizens, rendering true and accurate the false generic of his original "rights of man," the program of social reform Wollstonecraft outlines falls far short of gender equity, particularly in the field of public action. Although Wollstonecraft asserts woman's equal capacity for rationality, this is a potential that history has not allowed her to realize: "[T]hat woman is naturally weak, or degraded by a concurrence of circumstances, is, I think, clear" (141). Woman as Wollstonecraft finds her is more than likely to be driven by the passions that rationality should control. She should be educated and her mind developed so that it may learn to rule the body, but at present she is depraved and irrational. *Rights of Woman* deploys the egalitarian theory of natural rights as the underpinnings for a doctrine of differential gender capacity in separate spheres: Wollstonecraft's reformed women are naturally inclined to be wives and mothers, not stateswomen.

4. Wollstonecraft's troubled relation to both rationality and the feminine has proved a fruitful field of debate for feminist critics; the internal contradictions of *Rights* are such that neither Susan Gubar's epithet "feminist misogynist" ("Feminist Misogyny: Mary Wollstonecraft and the Paradox of 'It Takes One to Know One'") nor claims of Wollstonecraft's occupation of radical feminine otherness can encompass her position. While the political program of *Rights* is reformist at best, Wollstonecraft is always more rhetorically interesting than any examination of either her proposals or her account of female possibility might suggest. The desire for something more than peaceful occupation of republican womanhood, whether it be evidenced in momentary privileging of linguistic chaos, or ventriloquistic declamation of the rational language of the bourgeois citizen, constantly

reerupts on the surface of a circular, inconclusive text. The various compelling and competing readings provided by Cora Kaplan, Mary Jacobus, and Mary Poovey, among others, reenact a dialectic between authorization (Wollstonecraft as enabling foremother) and delegitimization (Wollstonecraft as outmoded precursor) that mirrors the text's own relation to its Painite, rationalist origins.(See, respectively, Kaplan, "Pandora's Box"; Jacobus, *Reading Woman*; and Poovey, *The Proper Lady and the Woman Writer*.)

5. For an extended version of the argument that Wollstonecraft's work is crucially formed by her inability to inhabit rational discourse and thus comfortably to engage a male audience in the absence of a female one, see my "Mary Wollstonecraft and the Search for the Radical Woman."

6. Eleanor Flexner, *Mary Wollstonecraft: A Biography*, 246.

7. Janet Todd and Marilyn Butler, eds., *The Works of Mary Wollstonecraft*, Vol. 7, 308.

8. Fanny Burney, *Evelina*, 8.

9. Jane West, *A Gossip's Story*, 2.

10. For a discussion of women writers' attempts to manipulate the jacobin novel as a radical instrument, see Eleanor Ty, *Unsex'd Revolutionaries*.

11. Several jacobin novels were published in 1796. Godwin's *St. Leon* (1799), which by some definitions is part of the genre, is the only other significant belated example of which I am aware. Generally speaking, by the end of the decade erstwhile radicals were either silent or had begun, like Maria Edgeworth, to write mild versions of anti-jacobin novels.

12. Mary Poovey's account of *Wrongs* in *The Proper Lady* sees the generic expectations of the novel of sensibility as overwhelming any politicizing possibility; Wollstonecraft, along with her heroine, is a willing victim of patriarchal, capitalist ideology that drowns female subjectivity in a fantasy of sexual empowerment that is always also submission. I will argue that the turn to sentiment is not a failure of political nerve, but a renewed attempt to find political purchase in a public sphere made slippery by conservative panic. Other readings, while also identifying *Wrongs* with retreat, seek to rescue the novel from Poovey's strictures by finding the return to sexuality a revalidation of the female body abjected in *Rights*. But I read the novel as a restaging of an essentially political battle; if the body is the site of contestation, it is a body politic as well as a body private that is in question. For the claim that *Wrongs* is Wollstonecraft's most radical text, see Jennifer Lorch, *Mary Wollstonecraft: The Making of a Radical Feminist*.

13. Mary Wollstonecraft, *The Wrongs of Woman*, 73. Subsequent quotations from this work are cited parenthetically in the text.

14. William Godwin, *Caleb Williams*, 1.

15. Tillotama Rajan, "Wollstonecraft and Godwin: Reading the Secrets of the Political Novel."

16. William Godwin, *Memoirs*, 154.

17. Ibid., 149.

18. This is not a program Wollstonecraft herself would have initiated, or possibly even condoned. The *Rights of Woman* has much to say about the education of women, and about how women's lives and the state of the nation might both be improved by women's aspiration to and attainment of universal standards of

knowledge and conduct—universal standards that are in fact those already in place for the education of men. Wollstonecraft's program of reform is based on no revolutionary reordering but on a gradualist model that does not contest an existing scheme of values: as far as the education and behavior of the model citizen is concerned, whatever is for men, is right. That Wollstonecraft could be seen to be diminishing the distinction between the sexes causes negative comment in 1792, but the disturbance is contained by the fact that masculine standards remain the absolutes toward which women might strive. Godwin's model, on the other hand, removes that unquestioned standard and reverses the hierarchy: rather than the absurd hyena that tries and fails to be a man—Wollstonecraft according to Walpole—the *Memoirs* produce a degendered paragon whom men and women alike should aspire to emulate. Where Wollstonecraft's *Rights of Woman* leaves absolutes unquestioned, suggesting that the circle of inclusion be widened but leaving those within in place, the place of superiority, Godwin's hagiographic account of Wollstonecraft's life works to render questionable all such givens. While Godwin divides individual intellectual attributes along gender lines, all social demarcation of gender is absent. This is a leap not present in Wollstonecraft's *Rights of Woman*, where social duties continue to be gender-defined. By suggesting that Wollstonecraft's life "as it was" needed no apology, notwithstanding and indeed to some extent because it departed from accepted practice, Godwin gives a more radical representation of Wollstonecraft to the public than can be construed from her *Vindications*.

Although feminist critics have read the reception of the *Memoirs* as indicating the threat represented by Wollstonecraft's theories played out in the real world, the *Memoirs* reveal not so much the naked Wollstonecraft—the secret uncovered—as yet another construction, and this one also not Wollstonecraft's own, but Godwin's.

19. Richard Polwhele, *The Unsex'd Females*, 29–30.

20. Review of *Memoirs*, *Monthly Visitor*, 241.

21. Ibid., 240.

22. George Preedy, *This Shining Woman*, 312; Claire Tomalin, *The Life and Death of Mary Wollstonecraft*, 202.

23. It is worth noting that this representation of Wollstonecraft as ravening hyena is historically specific; while the dangerous, sexually promiscuous image of this period is the one that came down to posterity, it should be understood as the product of a particular moment and its literature, the anti-jacobin panic. In 1792, even conservative reviews of *Rights of Woman* treat Wollstonecraft as a participant in civilized dialogue. The public sphere is a refined salon where witticisms are exchanged: "[A]s this is the first female combatant in the new field of the Rights of Woman, if we smile only, we shall be accused of wishing to decline the contest; if we content ourselves with paying a compliment to her talents, it will be styled inconsistent with "true dignity," and as showing that we want to continue the "slavish dependence."—We must contend then with this new Atalanta; and who knows whether, in this modern instance, we may not gain two victories by the contest? There is more than one batchelor in our corps; and, if we should *succeed*, miss Wollstonecraft may take her choice," Review of *Rights of Woman*, *Critical Review*, 390.

While misguided, Wollstonecraft has not been cast out from the circle of the mannered: she remains here someone with whom one may reasonably exchange views and even vows, albeit that the latter is conditional upon her defeat and submission in the conversational lists. Defeat is itself readily conceivable because Wollstonecraft, while she may overreach, is assumed to be playing by a set of agreed cultural rules. It is after the decay of public debate, and the disintegration of any progressive public sphere, that Wollstonecraft as speaker can be seen only as monstrous anomaly.

24. Review of *A Letter to the Women of England*, 311.
25. Letter to the Editor, *Lady's Monthly Museum*, 434–35.
26. Ibid., 435.
27. Anne Mellor, "Joanna Baillie and the Counter-Public Sphere," 560.

Chapter 2. *The Women's Room* and the Fiction of Consciousness

Both epigraphs are from Lindsy Van Gelder, "A Year Later"; the second is from interviews Van Gelder conducted with readers of *The Women's Room*.

1. Sara Sanborn, "A Feminist Jacqueline Susann?" 34; Wendy Stevens, Review of *The Women's Room*, 19.

2. Van Gelder, "A Year Later," 43. Lisa Hogeland interprets *The Women's Room*'s reviewing history in *Ms* somewhat differently, arguing that Van Gelder's article is an example of the "pro-men feminism" typical of *Ms* at this time, and that French's antimale agenda is too radical for the magazine's cultural feminist line; see *Feminism and Its Fictions*, 90–93. I see Van Gelder's comments about the novel's fascination with men and women's relations to them as stemming from a radical feminist position of the time, the "pro-woman" line; from this latter perspective, the problem with French was not that she was antimale but that she was so much more interested in men than in women.

3. Marie Lauret, *Liberating Literature*, 86.

4. The rehabilitation of French's reputation has proceeded in step with a series of attacks on avant-garde writing and formalist critics. Rita Felski argues for the greater political relevance of realist fiction in *Beyond Feminist Aesthetics*, while both Lauret and Patricia Waugh (in *Metafiction*) claim that feminist realist fiction, rather than being formally naive, is in fact a sophisticated rewriting of traditional forms—although in both cases "realism" becomes something of a stretched category, incorporating what are arguably aspects of modernism. Waugh sees a progression beyond realism as ultimately desirable, however, leaving "the novel of liberation" as an important but passing stage in feminist fiction's development.

5. Hogeland's account of consciousness-raising novels, which treats *The Women's Room* only in passing, as one among many, is an exception to this; because *Feminism and Its Fictions* historicizes the form and places it in context, her work is able to focus much more precisely on how texts operated in their original reading scene.

6. But I also share Susannah Radstone's skepticism about the significance and

agency of that shift of consciousness: "Changes in our lives *together with The Women's Room* form part of a shift from one femininity to another, with our lives forming part of a transition which, given the benefit of a wider historical perspective, we might neither welcome nor . . . celebrate [original italics]," "Introduction: Sweet Dreams and the Perverse Imagination," 12.

7. The definition of "bestseller" shifts with changes in how the publishing industry is organized. Richard Ohmann notes in "The Shaping of a Canon" that Robert Escarpit's 1966 formulation based on a book "finding" a series of audiences has been overtaken by multinationals' acquisition of publishers, a trend that began in the 1970s. Books are now explicitly targeted at particular, large, markets. Resa Dudovitz defines a bestseller in *The Myth of Superwoman* as "a book whose success . . . is manipulated and engineered in advance of its release"—a definition that certainly fits *Room*—but this sets up a false dichotomy between bestsellers and the rest which are, after all, also published in order to be sold. Peter Hohendahl points out in *The Institution of Criticism* that a bestseller must address topics that are currently hot in the public sphere; this essentially transient appeal is neatly captured in John Sutherland's definition: "the book that everyone is reading now, or that no one is reading anymore," *Bestsellers*, 31.

Prepublication publicity makes clear that *Room* was very thoroughly promoted and its success and dissemination arranged as far as possible. The notice in *Publisher's Weekly* of October 21, 1977 reads, in part: "Literary Guild alternate [choice], Warner's TV movie, big campaign." According to the *U.S Book Publishing Yearbook and Directory*, *Room* ranked tenth in the 1978 list for mass market bestsellers (2,200,000 copies in print) and ninth on the same list for 1979 (2,932,000 copies in print). Ahead of *Room* on the list in 1978 were, among others, *Jaws*, *The Thorn Birds*, and *The Amityville Horror*.

8. The attention paid to French—the creation of her as a celebrity in the mainstream media—was an exceptional treatment for a bestselling author at the time, but anticipates the status granted such authors in the more commodity-friendly conditions of the current book market.

French was interviewed twice for the *Times*, in November and December 1977. Two reviews appeared in the *Times*—one by Anne Tyler on October 16, 1977, and another by Christopher Lehmann-Haupt on October 27, 1977. The story about the paperback auction was widely covered in both trade papers and dailies. The *Times* carried a story in December 1977 about how Summit came to buy the manuscript, describing this transaction as "a Cinderella story."

9. Margaret Drabble, Review of *The Women's Room*.

10. Helen Yglesias, Review of *The Women's Room*.

11. Ibid.

12. In her article on the use of food metaphors in aesthetic disqualification, "Reading Is Not Eating," Janice Radway notes the totalizing effect of such metaphors, the reduction of words to consumable comfort. In the case of reviews of *The Women's Room*, however, it seems to me that something more complicated is happening: institutional reviewers wish *Room were* this kind of mere food, on the one hand, but they also seem to see some food as potentially enlivening, rather than tranquilizing, for its audience.

13. Christopher Lehmann-Haupt, Review of *The Women's Room*.

14. Review of *The Women's Room*, *Newsweek*.

15. Ibid.

16. Mme Defarge is a revolutionary in Dickens's *A Tale of Two Cities*; her knitting is used as a means of encoding subversive messages.

17. For celebrations and assessments of the role of feminist writing in sustaining and creating the women's liberation movement, see Lauret, *Liberating Literature* and Felski, *Beyond Feminist Aesthetics*. For the suggestion that the movement has decayed because fiction has failed to produce a feminist genre, see Maitland, "Futures in Feminist Fiction." For an account of the movement that suggests that the symbiosis of cultural production and political action might have negative consequences, see Jan Clausen, "A Movement of Poets" and Hogeland, *Feminism and Its Fictions*.

18. For an account of different feminist positions on the epistemological function of fiction, see Laura Marcus, "Feminist Aesthetics and the New Realism."

19. For an example of the debate held in terms of realism and modernism, see Toril Moi, *Sexual/Textual Politics*. While Felski's project in *Beyond Feminist Aesthetics* is to challenge the primacy of determining value through form, she also engages in a version of the same debate, privileging a reformed realism over an avant-garde version of modernism.

20. Modleski, *Loving with a Vengeance*, 30; Constance Penley, "Feminism, Psychoanalysis, and the Study of Popular Culture."

21. Janice Radway, *Reading the Romance*.

22. Quoted from interviews with readers in Van Gelder, "A Year Later," 44.

23. Dudovitz, *The Myth of Superwoman*, 5–6.

24. Hogeland's history of consciousness-raising, and of its move from activist counter-public sphere beginnings into the mainstream, in *Feminism and Its Fictions*, argues that with this move consciousness-raising lost its original purpose, "theory-building," and thus its collective resonances, becoming merely a means to personal growth. This seems to me accurate, but it is also clear—from, for instance, the remarks made by French that I quote here—that the *intention* to retain the possibilities for social change and action persisted. French clearly thought that her novel would incite changes on both individual and institutional levels, despite its status as mass market text.

25. French, Interview, *New York Times*, 4 November 1977.

26. French, quoted in Van Gelder, "A Year Later," 44.

27. Rosalind Coward, "Are Women's Novels Feminist Novels?" 234.

28. Ibid., 225, 237.

29. Hogeland makes a similar point in her critique of feminism's belief that what Hogeland calls "feminist literacy" would of itself be sufficient to produce social change; see *Feminism and Its Fictions*, "Feminism and/as Literacy."

30. For a particularly cogent and informed account of the connections between feminist thought and earlier radical movements, see Lauret, *Liberating Literature*, 47–54.

31. Quoted from interviews with readers in Van Gelder, "A Year Later," 43.

32. Ibid., 43–44.

33. See Nicci Gerrard, *Into the Mainstream*, 138.

34. For a reading of the film as a liberal reappropriation of a radical original, see Linda Blum, "Feminism and the Mass Media."

35. French, *The Women's Room*, 310–11. Subsequent quotations from this work are cited parenthetically in the text.

36. At the last moment, Dickens produces a personal, psychological trauma to motivate Mme DeFarge's revolutionary fervor; it turns out that her daughter was the victim of the *ancien régime*'s *droit de seigneur*.

CHAPTER 3. JODIE FOSTER SLAYS THE DRAGON: *THE ACCUSED* AND RAPE IN THE REEL WORLD

1. See, for example, Brian D. Johnson, "The Reality of Rape," for reviewers' transmission of the filmmakers' stated political purpose.

2. Laura Mulvey, "Visual Pleasure and Narrative Cinema," 11.

3. Teresa de Lauretis, *Alice Doesn't*, 67.

4. Tania Modleski, *The Woman Who Knew Too Much*, 4.

5. Unless otherwise indicated, quotations are taken from press coverage of the New Bedford case in *The Boston Globe*. Coverage of the public response to the case began on March 9, 1983, and continued through March 31. The trials opened on February 24, 1984, and coverage continued through March 27, when those found guilty were sentenced.

6. The quotations from interviews with neighbors in this paragraph are taken from coverage of the court proceedings in *The Boston Herald* in the first days of March, 1984, immediately following the victim's testimony.

7. For an alternative view, arguing that there was no conflict between ethnic and feminist positions other than that created by a racist media, see Lisa M. Cuklanz, "Public Expressions of 'Progress' in Discourses of the Big Dan's Rape."

8. Ellen Israel Rosen notes in "The New Bedford Rape Trial" that such repressive prescriptions of women's place became a way of defending and reaffirming the conservative traditional culture of the Azores (the place of origin of most recent Portuguese immigrants to New Bedford) against attack in an alien and racist environment.

9. Thus the prosecutor's closing argument to the jury was an invitation to scopic judgment with a particular focus: "You saw her with your own eyes, you could look at her, you could hear her. Did she have dignity? Did she have dignity?" Mr. Kane's Closing Argument, qtd. in Cuklanz, "Public Expressions," 9.

10. Elaine Scarry, *The Body in Pain*, 14.

11. Ibid., 16.

12. Patrice Fleck's reading of *The Accused* argues for the film's reformist and recuperative impulses; while I agree with this analysis, Fleck fails to take sufficient account of the elements of the film that run counter to the romance of judicial reward. Further, the narrative progression does produce another developmental process: as Sarah realizes that her own sense of returning self-worth will not itself change how others see her, so we realize that institutional change is necessary for social change. It is the dragon of community perception that must be slain, not by Sarah in her car, acting as an individual, but by Sarah in conjunction with the judicial system which alone has the power of redefinition. The film is thus aware

of, and centrally engages with, the issues of the production of meaning by and within institutional structures.

13. The triumph of the individual thus tends to operate against the film's own attempt to rewrite a wrong that it reveals as socially constructed. The way in which the film elides a conflict between different marginal discourses that operated as organizers of meaning in the New Bedford case illustrates the limitations of this strategy for refiguring actual local conditions. Since Sarah is a victim of both class and gender oppression, the film finds no conflict in producing a progressive program where both forms of inequity are addressed by Sarah's assumption of power. The removal of the issue of ethnic difference in the fictionalization of the New Bedford story and its replacement with class as an issue, an issue moreover between victim and authority rather than rapists and authority, enables a simple equation of underdog with moral right to remain in place. This elision allows the film to suggest that there is a natural, even inevitable, alliance between the sufferers of different forms of oppression. The narrative is accordingly able to propose as solution a traditional American individualist trajectory whereby the individual's path to self-determination is blocked by social forms that seek to limit the achievement of full potential. That self-assertion and the attempt to escape from institutionalized encoding as other and inferior may involve the substitution of another in the place of inferiority—as the Portuguese community protected its rights by attack on the victim and her rights as a woman—is thus repressed. The failure of the film to deal with the conflict between ethnic agendas and women's agendas exemplifies the limitations of a political strategy based on the assertion of individual rights, and the failure to recognize multiple locations of identity and power; thus *The Accused* must replicate the strategies of New Bedford by privileging one cause over another.

14. Various others have made this point, Patrice Fleck most extensively. Fleck argues that the film is always covertly not Sarah's but Ken's story, for not only is it his voiceover that brings about courtroom triumph, it is through his eyes that we see Sarah running from the bar in the opening sequence. That Sarah's authority is undermined by this structure, despite the film's claim to reestablish it, is confirmed by the dialogue between Sarah and her attorney as they wait for the verdict. A court official comes to tell them that the jury wants to hear Kenneth Joyce's testimony read to them for a third time. "Why not mine?" Sarah asks. "Because they believed you," Kathryn replies. Her response is intended to be affirming, both for Sarah and for the audience; it confirms that Sarah's credibility has indeed been established through the telling of her personal narrative. But what it also reveals is that the perceived truth of Sarah's story is irrelevant to the process of judgment; it is Ken's story that has the power to establish guilt or innocence, his word that will decree the verdict and thus, ultimately, the truth of Sarah's own.

15. Kaja Silverman, "Dis-Embodying the Female Voice," 131–32.

16. I am indebted to Jodie Foster's account of this scene: " '[Sarah] gets up to the stand in a good asexual outfit and says everything she was supposed to say, and does a good cross-examination . . . I wanted to be a face. And words. Period,' " "Interview," *New York Times*, 15.

17. Silverman, "Dis-Embodying the Female Voice," 134.

18. See Richard Corliss, " 'Bad' Women and Brutal Men."

19. Another way of addressing this question is to examine the agency or other-wise of the body on the pinball machine. It is, on a literal level at least, a body without words. The body without words can become a site of exchange. In their article "Up Against the Looking Glass!" Larry Riggs and Paula Willoquet suggest that *The Accused*, at the same time as anathematizing heterosexuality as male dom-inance, reveals the gang rape as an act of male homosexual communion. Sarah's body accordingly becomes, as they point out, merely a displaced site for the dis-play of homoerotic desire:

> Once she is forced down onto the pinball machine that is the altar for this rite, the woman disappears, except as the heterosexual pretext and alibi for an essentially homosexual ritual. Her mouth is covered, so her cries are not heard. Indeed, her capacity to produce signs or messages of any kind is virtually eliminated, since her arms are pinned down and even her eyes are covered most of the time. The cries and gestures of the "cele-brants" dominate absolutely. (219)

Riggs and Willoquet argue that to depict homosexual relations as those within which power and the creation and maintenance of social bonds are located *in itself* makes of woman an object of exchange, as if it were the feminist politics of the film that were responsible for Sarah's object status. They reach this position be-cause in their analysis the rape is also metonymic of heterosexuality: because the camera sees the sign of Danny's orgasm (facial contortions), what is represented must be the same, at least by association, as heterosexual intercourse. But if the film admits that rape is sex as well as violence (Danny's pleasure is expressed as orgasm rather than, say, as grunts of satisfaction accompanying a bludgeoning), this does not necessarily mean that it also suggests that all sex is rape. Rather the representation of the rape suggests that what is at issue here is the pursuit of violence by sexual means. Those sexual means require that the body disappear as *active agent;* it becomes invisible in some sense but it simultaneously becomes pure visibility, the passive site for representation and for reception of violence, sperm, and meaning. The disappearance of the body, then, is not only a result of its irrelevance to homosocial relations but also, due to its function as a rhetorical pivot, the point around which the argument turns. What matters in this scheme, to put it another way, is that we are looking, not what it is in particular we are looking at. In fact, the problem with the body on the pinball machine is that it is visible and invisible at the same time. As representation it generates various meanings (it is visible) but it cannot refer back to itself as locus of signification (it is invisible): it has meaning as a representation of a female body in cinema; as the object of the audience's voyeurism; as a site of exchange between participants. The body here generates meaning only for others, and not for itself—a passive object can acquire meaning, but it is meaning that is locked into the object and that can only be interpreted out of it by an active agent. It cannot know for itself or speak its own unmediated discourse.

20. Cindy Fuchs, Review of *The Accused*, 26–27.

21. de Lauretis, *Technologies of Gender*, 98.

22. Susanne Kappeler, *The Pornography of Representation*, 8.

CHAPTER 4. THE VISIBLE MARGIN: ANDRE LORDE AS I/ICON

An earlier version of this chapter appeared in *Women Poets of the Americas*, edited by Jacqueline Brogan and Cordelia Candelaria. © 1999 by University of Notre Dame Press. Reprinted with permission.

1. Hortense Spillers, "Afterword," *Conjuring*, 249–50.

2. Ibid., 250.

3. *Zami* was originally published by the short-lived Persephone Press, which, while it lasted, published only lesbian feminist titles; *Zami* was subsequently taken on by Crossing Press.

4. For example, a slightly altered extract from the text "Tar Beach" appeared in *Conditions* 5: *The Black Women's Issue*, 1979, a journal that describes itself as "a magazine of the writing by women, with an emphasis on the writing of lesbians."

5. I do not mean to suggest that any deliberate exclusion is at work here. Gloria Anzaldúa's *Borderlands/La Frontera* and Cherríe Moraga's *Loving in the War Years* are cited with at least equal frequency where the Other to be referenced is not specifically African-American but rather signifies the place of non-whiteness. That these three texts operate so persistently in the discourse of white feminist criticism as signifiers of difference suggests the extent to which that discourse circulates and recirculates between its users: each usage enables and requires the next.

While Susan Stanford Friedman locates *Zami* and *Borderlands* at different points in her taxonomy of "geographies of identity"—the first exemplifies the early form "multiple oppressions" while the second illustrates a later development of positional identity, "hybridity" (" 'Beyond' Gynocriticism and Gynesis," 17, 20)—all these works are routinely invoked as exemplary voices from the margin.

6. Robyn Wiegman identifies the critical operation whereby the margin is moved to the center as a "methodological fix" that does nothing to address social disempowerment (*American Anatomies*, 189). But what is at issue in Spillers's reading is not reading alone, but a shift in power relations stemming from the location of *Zami*'s production and reception.

7. Claudia Tate, ed., *Black Women Writers at Work*, 115.

8. Arguably, Friedman's use of *Zami* (" 'Beyond' Gynocriticism and Gynesis," 16–17) to exemplify a theoretical and subject position that goes "beyond" the gender-privileging of "gynocriticism" is an exception to this, but since *Zami* is described as producing Audre's identity as one of multiple jeopardies (which are also available to be read as multiple strengths), Lorde's text still occupies the position of the imperfect past which the present needs to modify.

9. In discussing *Zami*, I use "Audre" when referring to the protagonist, "Lorde" when referring to the author.

10. Barbara Smith, "The Truth That Never Hurts," 222. Smith's objection, for instance, to Gloria Naylor's portrayal of Black lesbians in *The Women of Brewster Place* is based on its unremitting hopelessness; in Smith's terms, Naylor's text has verisimilitude in its depiction of homophobia in the Black community but lacks authenticity because, after all, there is more to Black lesbian life than rape, madness, and self-hatred. Authenticity, in other words, is a projection of how life can

or could be lived. Only *Zami*, of the texts that Smith considers, achieves these qualities.

11. Ibid., 237.

12. In "Construing Truths in Lying Mouths: Truthtelling in Women's Autobiography," Sidonie Smith sets out the grounds of debate in contemporary feminist theory and practice. She lines up alternative sources of truth-telling, the essentialist "truth to experience" and the deconstructive "truth to ficticity of self" schools, oppositions that nonetheless imply a solution conceived of in terms of the possibility of absolute truth or its absence. Smith instead suggests that truth is relational, that the question to be asked is, Truth to what? Beginning from a notion of truth as both historically specific and constructed, she replaces the search for a determinate source for truth, or its replacement with an escape into ficticity, with a place of truth(s). If locations in time and space determine what we can know as true, then regimes of truth are multiple and can be contradictory, while the writer's relation to a regime, being relative, can be more or less contestatory. The autobiographer can thus to various degrees write herself into or out of (thus exposing the ficticity of) the truths of the moment.

13. Sidonie Smith, "Construing Truths in Lying Mouths," 163.

14. Audre Lorde, *Zami: A New Spelling of My Name*, 249. Subsequent quotations from this work are cited parenthetically in the text.

15. Alice Walker, "In Search of Our Mothers' Gardens," 237.

16. Christian presents this opinion somewhat tentatively, qualifying the claim with, "even as she admits her mother's disapproval of her and the differences between them," "No More Buried Lives," 199.

17. Lorde, *A Burst of Light*, 73.

18. Bonnie Zimmerman, "The Politics of Transliteration," 671–72.

19. Ibid., 682.

20. See, for example, Yvonne Klein's reading of *Zami* in "Myth and Community in Recent Lesbian Autobiographical Fiction."

21. John D'Emilio, who also writes about the bar of the time in *Sexual Politics, Sexual Communities*, gives a similar history, insofar as he too sees it as the first available public sphere for lesbians, but in his account it is a place of specifically working-class connection and identity formation. Lillian Faderman's analysis of his time in *Odd Girls and Twilight Lovers* is also organized around class differences: as a manifestation of lesbian existence, she claims, bars were avoided and organized against by middle-class lesbians. Rather than a place of communal identity, therefore, they functioned, according to Faderman, for middle-class lesbians as anathema, the identity to avoid, the difference not to be tolerated. (Lesbians joining Daughters of Bilitis [DOB], a middle-class organization, were required to conform not only to middle-class standards of behavior but also to heterosexual notions of femininity. The DOB project was assimilation through sameness, a project that involved among other things a particular dress code—looking like middle-class women rather than working-class men.)

22. For an extended account of how Lorde's rendering of the bar scene animates several eras of history simultaneously, see Katie King, "Audre Lorde's Lacquered Layerings."

23. This is also the definition given in JoAnn Loulan, *The Lesbian Erotic Dance*.

24. The emphasis of my reading is on finding oppositional possibility, rather than on positioning the subject and the text within the framework of identity politics. While such a politics is obviously crucial to Lorde's project, I am focusing less on where Lorde/Audre stands than on what use the text makes of such a positioning. In terms of the "geographies of identity" that Friedman maps out, the position I am suggesting here for Audre is one of relational identity, but not in precisely the form it takes in "'Beyond' Gynocriticism and Gynesis," since I read Audre's boundaries as temporary but impermeable, rather than fluid.

25. For a discussion of oppositional consciousness as political activism, see Chéla Sandoval, "Feminist Forms of Agency." See also Katie King, "Local and Global," for a critique of the utopian elements of Sandoval's position.

26. On feminists' changing the object of study as a necessary but insufficient activity, which she identifies as complicit with modernist teleological projects, despite its gloss of postmodernist multiplicity, see Wiegman, *American Anatomies*, 190.

27. For a range of examples of commentary on this phenomenon, see Margaret Homans, "Women of Color and Feminist Theory"; Toni Morrison, *Playing in the Dark*; Valerie Smith, "Black Feminist Theory and the Representation of the 'Other' "; and Elizabeth Abel, "Black Writing, White Reading: Race and the Politics of Feminist Interpretation." The articles by white feminist critics are also examples of the phenomenon in practice.

28. Jane Gallop, *Around 1981*, 169.

29. For a critique of Gallop's self-reflexivity, and of the exculpatory "I was blind but now I see" move, see Ann duCille, "The Occult of True Black Womanhood." For another response to Gallop's approach to "race," see Deborah McDowell, "Black Feminist Discourse: The 'Practice' of 'Theory,' " 107–11.

30. Wiegman makes the point that policing others' appropriations does not guarantee one's own noncomplicity in the process one would critique; she also suggests that to identify the history in question is to seek to construct oneself as "heroic interlope[r] into and reshape[r] of feminism's historical reinscriptions of white supremacy," *American Anatomies*, 189. The ubiquity of these kinds of interventions suggests to me, however, that rather than striking an heroic pose signifying difference, daring, and individual superiority, white feminist critics are falling into line, consciously joining an army already on the move.

31. See Mae Henderson, "Commentary on 'There Is No More Beautiful Way.' "

32. Ada Gay Griffin and Michelle Parkerson, *A Litany for Survival*. The film is currently available in two versions, as a ninety-minute film and a sixty-minute videotape. My descriptions, except where otherwise noted, refer to the latter. The shorter version has been re-edited, so that in addition to the excision of much material, the sequence of events has been changed.

33. Lorde, "The Master's Tools Will Never Dismantle the Master's House," in *Sister Outsider*.

34. While the film has not been widely distributed, it has been seen in many venues that are not all straightforwardly those of the counter-public sphere or for majority African-American audiences: for example, it was screened at the Sundance film festival, and an edited version was shown on PBS (June 18, 1996).

35. The information that Lorde refused to allow her ex-husband to be interviewed comes from a personal communication with Ada Gay Griffin.

36. The videotape's version of the speech, much reduced from the film original, omits Lorde's detailed account of the evildoings of New York State, including her reference to the military-industrial complex.

37. A particular example of this occurred at the first International Feminist Book Fair, held in London in 1984, where Lorde was scheduled to speak at a theater. Tickets sold out quickly, and Lorde came out on stage and asked the white women (it was a women-only event) in the audience to give up their seats to black women waiting outside, partly on the grounds that it was to them that she wished to speak, and partly because the location of the theater had made it harder for black women to get there. She then gave an address aimed very specifically at a black lesbian audience. I hadn't given up my seat, in what it will be clear is a long-running incapacity to come to terms with exclusion from Lorde's chosen audience.

38. See Lorde's acceptance speech on the occasion of her receiving an award from the Triangle Group at the Bill Whitehead Memorial Award Ceremony, 1990, "What Is at Stake in Lesbian and Gay Publishing Today."

39. This whole discussion is of course conducted in the awareness of the ways in which Lorde's presence in this text might itself be read as tokenism. That I think such presence justifiable, even if it must to some extent repeat what it would critique, should emerge in what follows.

40. Barbara Smith appears in the film both to make this point and to locate *The Cancer Journals* as a landmark text in the "truth-telling" that enabled this shift of consciousness.

AFTERWORD

1. Vladimir Nabokov, *Lolita*, 142.

2. Hogeland reads feminist use of *Thelma and Louise* differently: "The deployment of images from *Thelma and Louise* by mainstream feminists marks, I suggest, a specific historical moment of a very real sense of impotence, of powerlessness, that feminists felt in the early 1990s," *Feminism and Its Fictions*, 162–63. Rather than see misreadings of the film as markers of despair, however, I think they can be understood as creative oppositional tactics.

Works Cited

Abel, Elizabeth. "Black Writing, White Reading: Race and the Politics of Feminist Interpretation." *Critical Inquiry* 19 (spring 1993): 470–98.

The Accused. Dir. Jonathan Kaplan. With Jodie Foster, Kelly McGillis. Paramount Pictures, 1988.

Anzaldúa, Gloria. *Borderlands/La Frontera: The New Mestiza*. San Francisco: Spinsters/Aunt Lute, 1987.

Bage, Robert. *Hermsprong, Or Man As He Is Not*. 1796. Oxford: Oxford University Press, 1985.

Baker, Houston A. *Workings of the Spirit: The Poetics of Afro-American Women's Writing*. Chicago: University of Chicago Press, 1991.

Benhabib, Seyla. *Situating the Self: Gender, Community and Postmodernism in Contemporary Ethics*. London: Routledge, 1992.

Berlant, Lauren. "The Female Complaint." *Social Text* 19/20 (fall 1988): 237–59.

Bhabha, Homi K. "Interrogating Identity: The Postcolonial Perogative." In *The Anatomy of Racism*. Edited by David Theo Goldberg, 183–209. Minneapolis: University of Minnesota Press, 1990.

———, ed. *Nation and Narration*. London: Routledge, 1990.

Blum, Linda M. "Feminism and the Mass Media: A Case Study of *The Women's Room* as Novel and Television Film." *Berkeley Journal of Sociology* 27 (1982): 1–24.

Brown, Rita Mae. *Rubyfruit Jungle* New York: Daughters, Inc. 1973.

Burke, Edmund. *Reflections on the Revolution in France*. 1790. Harmondsworth, UK: Penguin, 1986.

Burney, Fanny. *Evelina*. 1778. Oxford: Oxford University Press, 1982.

Case, Sue-Ellen. "Toward a Butch-Feminist Retro-Future." In *Cross-Purposes: Lesbians, Feminists, and the Limits of Alliance*. Edited by Dana Heller, 205–20. Bloomington: Indiana University Press, 1997.

Chow, Rey. *Writing Diaspora: Tactics of Intervention in Contemporary Cultural Studies*. Bloomington: Indiana University Press, 1993.

Christian, Barbara. "No More Buried Lives: The Theme of Lesbianism in Audre Lorde's *Zami*, Gloria Naylor's *Women of Brewster Place*, Ntozake Shange's *Sassafras, Cypress and Indigo*, and Alice Walker's *The Color Purple*." In Barbara Christian, *Black Feminist Criticism*, 187–204. New York: Pergamon Press, 1985.

———. "The Race for Theory." *Feminist Studies* 14 (spring 1988): 67–79.

Clausen, Jan. "A Movement of Poets." 1982. Reprinted in Jan Clausen, *Books and Life*. Columbus: Ohio State University Press, 1989.

Corliss, Richard. " 'Bad' Women and Brutal Men." Review of *The Accused* (Paramount movie) *Time*, 21 November 1988, 126.

Coward, Rosalind. "Are Women's Novels Feminist Novels?" 1980. Reprinted in *The New Feminist Criticism*. Edited by Elaine Showalter. New York: Pantheon Books, 1985: 225–39.

Cuklanz, Lisa M. "Public Expressions of 'Progress' in Discourses of the Big Dan's Rape." *Women and Language* 17 (spring 1994): 1–12.

Davis, Madeline, and Elizabeth Lapovsky Kennedy. *Boots of Leather, Slippers of Gold: The History of a Lesbian Community*. New York: Routledge, 1993.

De Lauretis, Teresa. *Alice Doesn't: Feminism, Semiotics, Cinema*. Bloomington: Indiana University Press, 1984.

———. "Eccentric Subjects: Feminist Theory and Historical Consciousness." *Feminist Studies* 16 (spring 1990): 115–50.

———. *Technologies of Gender: Essays on Theory, Film, and Fiction*. Bloomington: Indiana University Press, 1987.

D'Emilio, John. *Sexual Politics, Sexual Communities: The Making of a Homosexual Minority in the United States, 1940–1970*. Chicago: University of Chicago Press, 1983.

Dickens, Charles. *A Tale of Two Cities*. London: Chapman and Hall, 1859.

Drabble, Margaret. Review of *The Women's Room*, *The Listener*, 20 April 1978, 508.

duCille, Ann. "The Occult of True Black Womanhood: Critical Demeanor and Black Feminist Studies." *Signs* 19 (1994): 591–629.

Dudovitz, Resa L. *The Myth of Superwoman: Women's Bestsellers in France and the U.S.* London: Routledge, 1990.

Duncker, Patricia. *Sisters and Strangers: An Introduction to Contemporary Feminist Fiction*. Oxford: Blackwell, 1992.

DuPlessis, Rachel Blau. *Writing Beyond the Ending: Narrative Strategies of Twentieth-Century Women Writers*. Bloomington: Indiana University Press, 1985.

Elam, Diane. *Feminism and Deconstruction: Ms. en Abyme*. New York: Routledge, 1994.

———, and Robyn Wiegman, eds. *Feminism Beside Itself*. New York: Routledge, 1995.

Escarpit, Robert. *The Book Revolution*. London: Harrap, 1966.

Faderman, Lillian. *Odd Girls and Twilight Lovers: A History of Lesbian Life in Twentieth-Century America*. New York: Columbia University Press, 1991.

Felski, Rita. *Beyond Feminist Aesthetics: Feminist Literature and Social Change*. Cambridge: Harvard University Press, 1989.

Fetterley, Judith. *The Resisting Reader: A Feminist Approach to American Literature*. Bloomington: Indiana University Press, 1978.

Fleck, Patrice. "The Silencing of Women in the Hollywood 'Feminist' Film: *The Accused*." *Post-Script* 9 (summer 1990): 49–55.

Flexner, Eleanor. *Mary Wollstonecraft: A Biography*. New York: Coward, McCann and Geoghegan, 1972.

Foster, Jodie. Interview by Sonia Taitz. *New York Times,* 16 October 1988, 15ff.

Foucault, Michel. *Discipline and Punish: The Birth of the Prison.* 1975. New York: Vintage, 1979.

French, Marilyn. *The Women's Room.* 1977. New York: Jove, 1978.

———. Interview by Nan Robertson. *New York Times,* 4 November 1977, 20.

———. Interview by Herbert Mitgang. *New York Times,* 25 December 1977, sec. 7, 7.

———. Interview by Janet Todd. In *Women Writers Talking,* ed. Janet Todd, 69–78. New York: Holmes and Meier, 1983.

———. "Is There a Feminine Aesthetic?" In *Aesthetics in Feminist Perspective,* ed. Hilde Hein and Carolyn Korsmeyer, 68–76. Bloomington: Indiana University Press, 1993.

Friedman, Susan Stanford. "Beyond White and Other: Relationality and Narratives of Race in Feminist Discourse." *Signs* 21 (1995): 1–47.

———. " 'Beyond' Gynocriticism and Gynesis: The Geographies of Identity and the Future of Feminist Criticism." *Tulsa Studies in Women's Literature* 15 (Spring 1996): 13–40.

Frye, Joanne S. *Living Stories, Telling Lives: Women and the Novel in Contemporary Experience.* Ann Arbor: University of Michigan Press, 1986.

Fuchs, Cindy. Review of *The Accused* (Paramount movie). *Cineaste* 17 (1989): 26–28.

Gallop, Jane. *Around 1981: Academic Feminist Literary Theory.* New York: Routledge, 1992.

Gardiner, Judith Kegan, ed. *Provoking Agents: Gender and Agency in Theory and Practice.* Urbana and Chicago: University of Illinois Press, 1995.

Gerrard, Nicci. *Into the Mainstream.* London: Pandora, 1989.

Godwin, William. *Memoirs of the Author of A Vindication of the Rights of Woman.* London: Joseph Johnson, 1798.

———. *St. Leon.* London, 1799.

———. *Things As They Are; or, The Adventures of Caleb Williams.* 1794. London: Penguin, 1988.

Greene, Gayle. *Changing the Story: Feminist Fiction and the Tradition.* Bloomington: Indiana University Press, 1991.

Griffin, Ada Gay, and Michelle Parkerson (dir.). *A Litany for Survival: The Life and Work of Audre Lorde.* New York: Third World Newsreel, 1995/1996. Film, videotape.

Gubar, Susan. "Feminist Misogyny: Mary Wollstonecraft and the Paradox of 'It Takes One to Know One.' " In *Feminism Beside Itself,* Edited by Diane Elam and Robyn Wiegman, 133–54.

———. "What Ails Feminist Criticism?" *Critical Inquiry* 24 (summer 1998): 878–902.

———. "Notations in Media Res." *Critical Inquiry* 25 (winter 1999): 380–96.

Henderson, Mae. "Response to 'There Is No More Beautiful Way: Theory and the Poetics of Afro-American Women's Writing,' by Houston Baker." In *Afro-American Literary Studies in the 1990s*, Edited by Houston A. Baker, Jr., and Patricia Redmond, 155–63. Chicago: University of Chicago Press, 1989.

Hite, Molly. *The Other Side of the Story: Structures and Strategies of Contemporary Feminist Narrative*. Ithaca: Cornell University Press, 1989.

Hogeland, Lisa Maria. *Feminism and Its Fictions: The Consciousness-Raising Novel and the Women's Liberation Movement*. Philadelphia: University of Pennsylvania Press, 1998.

Hohendahl, Peter U. *The Institution of Criticism*. Ithaca: Cornell University Press, 1982.

Holcroft, Thomas. *Anna St. Ives*. London, 1792.

Homans, Margaret. "Her Very Own Howl: The Ambiguities of Representation in Recent Women's Fiction." *Signs* 9 (winter 1983): 186–205.

———. " 'Racial Composition': Metaphor and the Body in the Writing of Race." In *Female Subjects in Black and White: Race, Psychoanalysis, Feminism*. Edited by Elizabeth Abel et al., 77–101. Berkeley and Los Angeles: University of California Press, 1997.

———. "Women of Color and Feminist Theory," *NLH* 25 (1994): 73–94.

Howe, Florence, et al. "Books That Changed Our Lives." Panel at Modern Language Association Convention, Chicago, December 1990. Reprinted in *Women's Studies Quarterly*, 19, 3–4 (1991): 9–40.

Jacobs, Harriet. Incidents in the Life of a Slave Girl. 1861. Cambridge: Harvard University Press, 1987.

Jacobus, Mary. *Reading Woman: Essays in Feminist Criticism*. New York: Columbia University Press, 1986.

Johnson, Brian D. "The Reality of Rape." Review of *The Accused* (Paramount movie). *Macleans'*, 24 October 1988, 60–62.

Kaplan, Carey, and Ellen Cronan Rose, eds. *The Canon and the Common Reader*. Knoxville: University of Tennessee Press, 1990.

Kaplan, Cora. "Feminist Criticism Twenty Years On." In *From My Guy to Sci-Fi: Genre and Women's Writing in the Postmodern World*. Edited by Helen Carr, 15–23. London: Pandora, 1989.

———. "Pandora's Box: Subjectivity, Class, and Sexuality in Socialist Feminist Criticism." In *Making a Difference: Feminist Literary Criticism*, ed. Gayle Greene and Coppélia Kahn, 146–76. London: Methuen, 1985.

Kappeler, Susanne. *The Pornography of Representation*. Minneapolis: University of Minnesota Press, 1986.

King, Katie. "Audre Lorde's Lacquered Layerings: The Lesbian Bar as a Site of Literary Production." In *The New Lesbian Criticism*. Edited by Sally Munt, 51–74.

———. "Local and Global: AIDS Activism and Feminist Theory." In *Provoking Agents*, ed. Judith Kegan Gardiner, 93–112.

Klein, Yvonne. "Myth and Community in Recent Lesbian Autobiographical Fiction." In *Lesbian Texts and Contexts: Radical Revisions*, Edited by Karla Jay, Joanne

Glasgow, and Catharine R. Stimpson, 330–38. New York: New York University Press, 1990.

Kuhn, Annette. *Women's Pictures: Feminism and Cinema*. London: Routledge, 1982.

Landes, Joan. *Women and the Public Sphere in the Age of the French Revolution*. Ithaca: Cornell University Press, 1988.

Lauret, Marie. *Liberating Literature: Feminist Fiction in America*. New York: Routledge, 1994.

Lehmann-Haupt, Christopher. Review of *The Women's Room*, by Marilyn French. *New York Times*, 27 October 1977, sec. 4, 15.

Letter to the Editor. *Lady's Monthly Museum* (December 1799): 433–36.

Lorch, Jennifer. *Mary Wollstonecraft: The Making of a Radical Feminist*. Oxford: Berg, 1990.

Lorde, Audre. *A Burst of Light*. Ithaca, NY: Firebrand Books, 1988.

———. *The Cancer Journals*. Argyle, NY: Spinsters Ink, 1980.

———. *Sister Outsider*. Trumansburg, NY: Crossing Press, 1984.

———. "What Is at Stake in Lesbian and Gay Publishing Today." *Callaloo* 14 (winter 1991): 65–66.

———. *Zami: A New Spelling of My Name*. Watertown, MA: Persephone, 1982.

Loulan, JoAnn. *The Lesbian Erotic Dance: Butch, Femme, Androgyny, and Other Rhythms*. San Francisco: Spinsters Ink, 1990.

Mailloux, Steven. *Reception Histories: Rhetoric, Pragmatism, and American Cultural Politics*. Ithaca: Cornell University Press, 1998.

———. *Rhetorical Power*. Ithaca: Cornell University Press, 1989.

Maitland, Sara. "Futures in Feminist Fiction." In *From My Guy to Sci-Fi: Genre and Women's Writing in the Postmodern World*. Edited by Helen Carr, 193–203. London: Pandora, 1989.

Marcus, Laura. "Feminist Aesthetics and the New Realism." In *New Feminist Discourses: Critical Essays on Theories and Texts*, Edited by Isobel Armstrong, 11–25. London: Routledge, 1992.

McDowell, Deborah. "Black Feminist Discourse: The 'Practice' of 'Theory.' " In *Feminism Beside Itself*. Edited by Elam and Wiegman, 93–118.

Mellor, Anne. "Joanna Baillie and the Counter-Public Sphere." *Studies in Romanticism* 33 (winter 1994): 559–67.

Modleski, Tania. *Loving With a Vengeance: Mass-Produced Fantasies for Women*. London: Methuen, 1984.

———. *The Woman Who Knew Too Much: Hitchcock & Feminist Theory*. New York: Methuen, 1988.

Mohanty, Chandra Talpade. "Under Western Eyes: Feminist Scholarship and Colonial Discourses. In *Contemporary Postcolonial Theory: A Reader*. Edited by Padmini Mongia. London: Edward Arnold, 1996.

Moi, Toril. *Sexual/Textual Politics: Feminist Literary Theory*. London: Methuen, 1985.

Moraga, Cherríe. *Loving in the War Years*. Boston: South End Press, 1983.

————, and Gloria Anzaldúa, eds. *This Bridge Called My Back: Writings by Radical Women of Color*. Watertown, MA: Persephone, 1981.

Morrison, Toni. *Playing in the Dark: Whiteness and the Literary Imagination*. Cambridge: Harvard University Press, 1992.

Mulvey, Laura. "Visual Pleasure and Narrative Cinema." *Screen* 16 (autumn 1975): 6–18.

Munt, Sally, ed. *The New Lesbian Criticism*. New York: Columbia University Press, 1992.

Nabokov, Vladimir. *Lolita*. 1955. New York: Viking, 1992.

Naylor, Gloria. *The Women of Brewster Place*. New York: Viking, 1982.

Nicholson, Linda J., ed. *Feminism/Postmodernism*. New York: Routledge, 1990.

Ohmann, Richard. "The Shaping of a Canon: U.S. Fiction 1960–1975." *Critical Inquiry* 10 (1983): 199–223.

Paris Is Burning. Dir. Jenni Livingston. Off White Productions, 1990.

Penley, Constance. "Feminism, Psychoanalysis, and the Study of Popular Culture." In *Cultural Studies*. Edited by Lawrence Grossberg et al., 479–94. New York: Routledge, 1992.

Polwhele, Richard. *The Unsex'd Females. A Poem: Addressed to the Author of The Pursuits of Literature*. London, 1798.

Poovey, Mary. *The Proper Lady and the Woman Writer: Ideology as Style in the Works of Mary Wollstonecraft, Mary Shelley, and Jane Austen*. Chicago: University of Chicago Press, 1984.

Preedy, George. *This Shining Woman*. London: Collins, 1937.

Pryse, Marjorie, and Hortence Spillers, eds. *Conjuring: Black Women, Fiction, and Literary Tradition*. Bloomington: Indiana University Press, 1985.

Radstone, Susannah. "Introduction: Sweet Dreams and the Perverse Imagination." In *Sweet Dreams: Sexuality, Gender and Popular Fiction*. Edited by Susannah Radstone, 9–19. London: Lawrence & Wishart, 1988.

Radway, Janice. *Reading the Romance: Women, Patriarchy, and Popular Culture*. Chapel Hill: University of North Carolina Press, 1984.

————. "Reading Is Not Eating: Mass Produced Literature and the Theoretical, Methodological and Political Consequences of a Metaphor." *Book Research Quarterly* 2 (1986): 7–29.

Rajan, Tillotama. "Wollstonecraft and Godwin: Reading the Secrets of the Political Novel." *Studies in Romanticism* 27 (1988): 221–51.

Rapping, Elaine. "Liberation in Chaos: 'The Woman Question' in Hollywood." *Cineaste* 17 (1989): 4–11.

Reagon, Bernice Johnson. "Coalition Politics: Turning the Century." In *Home Girls: A Black Feminist Anthology*. Edited by Barbara Smith, 356–68. New York: Kitchen Table/Women of Color Press, 1983.

Review of *A Letter to the Women of England on the Injustice of Mental Subordination; with Anecdotes*, by Anne-Francis Randall. *Gentleman's Magazine*, April 1799, 311.

Review of *Memoirs of the Author of A Vindication of the Rights of Woman*, by William Godwin. *Monthly Review* (November 1798): 321–7.

Review of Memoirs of the Author of A Vindication of the Rights of Woman, by William Godwin. Monthly Visitor (March 1798): 240–41.

Review of *A Vindication of the Rights of Woman*, by Mary Wollstonecraft. *Analytical Review* (March 1792): 241–49.

Review of *A Vindication of the Rights of Woman*, by Mary Wollstonecraft. *Critical Review* 4 (April 1792): 389–98; 5 (June 1792): 132–42.

Review of *A Vindication of the Rights of Woman*, by Mary Wollstonecraft. *Monthly Review* (June 1792): 198–209.

Review of *The Women's Room*, by Marilyn French. *Newsweek*, 24 October 1977, 121.

Review of *The Women's Room*, by Marilyn French. *Publisher's Weekly*, 29 August 1977, 354.

Riggs, Larry W., and Paula Willoquet. "Up Against the Looking Glass! Homosexual Epiphany in *The Accused.*" *Literature and Film Quarterly* 17 (October 1989): 214–23.

Rose, Ellen Cronan. "Review Essay: American Feminist Criticism of Contemporary Women's Fiction." *Signs* 18 (1993): 346–75.

Rosen, Ellen Israel. "The New Bedford Rape Trial: New Thoughts on an Old Problem." *Dissent* 32 (1985): 207–12.

Rubenstein, Roberta. *Boundaries of the Self: Gender, Culture, Fiction.* Champaign: University of Illinois Press, 1987.

Sage, Lorna. *Women in the House of Fiction: Post-War Women Novelists.* Basingstoke, UK: Macmillan, 1992.

Sanborn, Sara. "A Feminist Jacqueline Susann?" Review of *The Women's Room*, by Marilyn French. *Ms.*, January 1978, 30, 34.

Sandoval, Chéla. "U.S. Third World Feminism: The Theory and Method of Oppositional Consciousness in the Postmodern World." *Genders* 10 (spring 1991): 1–24.

———. "Feminist Forms of Agency and Oppositional Consciousness: U.S. Third World Feminism." In *Provoking Agents.* Edited by Judith Kegan Gardiner, 208–26.

Scarry, Elaine. *The Body in Pain: The Making and Unmaking of the World.* New York: Oxford University Press, 1985.

Silverman, Kaja. "Dis-Embodying the Female Voice." In *Re-vision: Essays in Feminist Film Criticism,* Edited by Mary Ann Doane, Patricia Mellencamp, and Linda Williams, 131–49. Los Angeles: University Press of America, 1984.

Smith, Barbara. "The Truth That Never Hurts: Black Lesbians in Fiction in the 1980s." In *Wild Women in the Whirlwind: Afra-American Culture and the Contemporary Literary Renaissance.* Edited by Joanne M. Braxton and Andrée Nicola Mclaughlin, 213–45. New Brunswick, NJ: Rutgers University Press, 1990.

Smith, Sidonie. "Construing Truths in Lying Mouths: Truthtelling in Women's Autobiography." *Studies in Literary Imagination* 23 (fall 1990): 145–63.

Smith, Valerie. "Black Feminist Theory and the Representation of the 'Other.' "

In *Changing Our Own Words: Essays on Criticism, Theory, and Writing by Black Women,* ed. Cheryl A. Wall, 38–57. New Brunswick, NJ: Rutgers University Press, 1989.

Spillers, Hortense. "Afterword: Cross-Currents, Discontinuities: Black Women's Fiction." In *Conjuring.* Edited by Marjorie Pryse and Hortense Spillers, 249–61.

Stevens, Wendy. Review of *The Women's Room,* by Marilyn French. *off our backs,* February 1978, 18–19.

Sutherland, John. *Bestsellers: Popular Fiction of the 1970s.* London: Routledge, 1981.

Tate, Claudia, ed. *Black Women Writers at Work.* Harpenden, UK: Oldcastle Books, 1985.

Thelma and Louise. Dir. Ridley Scott. MGM Pictures, 1991.

Tomalin, Claire. *The Life and Death of Mary Wollstonecraft.* London: Weidenfeld and Nicolson, 1974.

Ty, Eleanor. *Unsex'd Revolutionaries: Five Women Novelists of the 1790s.* Toronto: University of Toronto Press, 1993.

U.S. Book Publishing Yearbook and Directory, 1979–80. White Plains, NY: Knowledge Industry Publications, 1979.

Van Gelder, Lindsy. "A Year Later: The Lure of *The Women's Room.*" *Ms,* April 1979, 42–44.

Walker, Alice. "In Search of Our Mothers' Gardens." 1983. Reprinted in *In Search of Our Mothers' Gardens: Womanist Prose.* London: The Women's Press, 1984.

Waugh, Patricia. *Metafiction: The Theory and Practice of Self-Conscious Fiction.* London: Methuen, 1984.

———. *Feminine Fictions: Revisiting the Postmodern.* New York: Routledge, 1989.

West, Jane. *A Gossip's Story.* London, 1798.

Wicke, Jennifer, and Margaret Ferguson, eds. *Feminism and Postmodernism.* Durham and London: Duke University Press, 1994.

Wiegman, Robyn. *American Anatomies: Theorizing Race and Gender.* Durham and London: Duke University Press, 1995.

———. "What Ails Feminist Criticism: A Second Opinion." *Critical Inquiry* 25 (winter 1999): 362–79.

Williams, Raymond. *Marxism and Literature.* Oxford: Oxford University Press, 1977.

Wilson, Anna. "Death and the Mainstream: Lesbian Detective Fiction and the Killing of the Coming-Out Story." *Feminist Studies* 22 (summer 1996): 251–78.

———. "Mary Wollstonecraft and the Search for the Radical Woman." *Genders* 6 (1989): 88–101.

Wilson, Elizabeth. "Tell It Like It Is: Women and Confessional Writing." In *Sweet Dreams.* Edited by Susannah Radstone, 21–45.

Wollstonecraft, Mary. *A Vindication of the Rights of Woman.* 1792. London: Penguin, English Library, 1982.

————. *Mary and The Wrongs of Woman*. Edited by Gary Kelly. Oxford: Oxford University Press, 1980.

————. *The Works of Mary Wollstonecraft*. 7 vols. Edited by Janet Todd and Marilyn Butler. London: William Pickering, 1989.

Yglesias, Helen. Review of *The Women's Room*, by Marilyn French. *Harper's*, January 1978, 84.

Zimmerman, Bonnie. "The Politics of Transliteration: Lesbian Personal Narratives." *Signs* 9 (1984): 663–82.

Index

Abel, Elizabeth, 114, 116
Accused, The, 24, 71–73, 76–94, 128; analysis of class in, 79, 142 n. 13; as attempting to change its audience, 72, 77, 84, 85–88, 90–92; as feminist text, 16, 71, 82; as intervention in New Bedford rape case, 71–72, 82, 93–94; as narrative of recovery of self, 78–83, 141 n. 12; problem of objectification of female subject in, 71–72, 84, 88–91, 142 n.14, 143 n. 19; rape scene in, 83–86, 143 n. 19; reception of, 85, 86–88. *See also* New Bedford rape case
Analytical Review, 30
Anti-jacobin novel: dominance of 31; purpose of, 30; written by former jacobins, 136 n. 11
Anzaldúa, Gloria, 144 n. 5

Bage, Robert, 31
Baker, Houston, 117
Bestseller, definition of, 139 n.7. See also *The Women's Room*
Big Dan rape case: *See* New Bedford rape case; *Accused, The*
Blum, Linda, 140 n. 34
Breast cancer: as disproportionately affecting African Americans, 126; in feminist discourse, 125–26
Brown, Rita Mae, 21
Burst of Light, A (Lorde), 119
Butler, Judith, 116, 133 n. 16
Burke, Edmund, 30
Burney, Fanny, 30

Cancer Journals, The (Lorde), 118, 119
Canon, revision of: by African-American women writers, 96, 103, 113; to exclude political fiction, 29–30; by feminist criticism, 13, 15; in women's studies, 129–30
Case, Sue-Ellen, 134 n. 26
Christian, Barbara, 103, 105, 145 n. 16
Clausen, Jan, 133 n. 14, 140 n. 17
CNN, 74
Conditions, 144 n. 4
Consciousness-raising: by *The Accused*, 91–92; by fiction, 14–15, 58–9, 133 n. 12, 138 n. 5; by group compared to individual reading, 61, 68; by Hitchcock films, 133 n. 15; Marxist feminist critique of, 59–60; mechanics of, 57–58; move into mainstream of, 140 n. 24; political antecedents of, 60
Counter-public sphere, 20–22, 95; in 1790s, 45–46; Lorde's work located in, 24–25; as site of production, 55–56, 97; shifting boundaries of, 21; as site of resistance, 21, 95–96; *The Women's Room* in, 24, 47–48. *See also* Public sphere
Coward, Rosalind, 59–60
Critical Review: reception of *Vindication of the Rights of Woman*, 137 n.23
Cuklanz, Lisa, 141 n. 7

Daughters of Bilitis, membership of, 145 n. 21. *See also* Lesbians
Davis, Madeline, 110
De Lauretis, Teresa: theory of split subject, 18; on filmic mechanisms, 72, 90
D'Emilio, John: on history of lesbian bars, 145 n. 21
duCille, Ann, 146 n. 28

157

New Bedford rape case, 74–77, 92–93; effect of trial, 92–93; media coverage of, 74–75; protest marches generated by, 75–76; and racism, 75–76, 141 nn. 7 and 8, 142 n. 13; response of community to victim, 74–76; role of onlookers in, 74. See also *The Accused*
Newsweek, 52
New York Times, 49, 51

Ohmann, Richard, 139 n. 7

Paine, Thomas, 27
Paris is Burning (Livingston), 73
Parkerson, Michelle, 146 n. 32
Penley, Constance, 56
Polwhele, Richard: response to Wollstonecraft, 42
Poovey, Mary: on sensibility, 136 n. 12
Pryse, Marjorie, 115
Public sphere: anti-jacobin, 43, 46; exclusion of women from, 27, 29; 70s feminist writers' relation to, 46; novel as means of entry to, 29, 31, 45; reading of oppositional texts in, 23–24; relation to counter-public sphere, 20–21; Wollstonecraft in, 23, 29. See also Counter-public sphere

Radstone, Susannah: on feminist myths of transformation, 133 n. 11, 138 n. 6
Radway, Janice, 139 n. 12; and romance reading as resistance, 56
Rajan, Tillotama, 34–35, 38
Reagon, Bernice Johnson, 127
Republican womanhood, 27–28, 135 n. 3
Resistance, location of, 12–13, 17–22; Lorde as figure of, 116–17, 118; in mass market fiction, 56
Rich, Adrienne, 124
Riggs, Larry, 143 n. 19
Rights of Man (Paine), 27
Rights of Woman (Wollstonecraft). See

Vindication of the Rights of Woman; Wollstonecraft
Rose, Ellen Cronan, 14–15
Rosen, Ellen Israel, 141 n. 8

Sanchez, Sonia, 122
Sandoval, Chéla, 22, 146 n. 25
Scarry, Elaine, 78, 92
Silverman, Kaya, 83–84
Smith, Barbara, 100–101, 102, 144 n. 10, 147 n. 40
Smith, Sidonie, 101–3; theory of autobiographical subject, 145 n. 12
Smith, Valerie, 114
Spillers, Hortense, 115; on African-American women's literary production, 96–97
Stowe, Harriet Beecher, 128

Tallyrand, 29
Thelma and Louise (Scott), 130–31, 147 n. 2
Topor, Tom, 71, 86
Ty, Eleanor, 136 n. 10

Uncle Tom's Cabin (Stowe), 128

Vindication of the Rights of Man (Wollstonecraft), 26, 32
Vindication of the Rights of Woman (Wollstonecraft), 23, 26–29, 31–32, 34, 35, 44, 62; original reception of, 137 n. 23; political program of, 27–28, 135 nn. 3 and 4, 136 nn. 5 and 18; responses of feminist critics to, 135 n. 4; rhetorical strategies of, 27–29
Van Gelder, Lindsy, 47

Walker, Alice, construction of matrilineal tradition, 103
West, Jane, 30
Wiegman, Robin: critique of gender focused criticism, 133 n. 16; critique of white-focused criticism, 134 n. 17, 144 n. 6, 146 nn. 26 and 30
Williams, Raymond, 20
Wilson, Elizabeth, 19